Freud at 150

Freud at 150

21st-Century Essays on a Man of Genius

Edited by Joseph P. Merlino, Marilyn S. Jacobs,
Judy Ann Kaplan, K. Lynne Moritz

A JASON ARONSON BOOK

ROWMAN & LITTLEFIELD PUBLISHERS, INC.
Lanham • Boulder • New York • Toronto • Plymouth, UK

A JASON ARONSON BOOK

ROWMAN & LITTLEFIELD PUBLISHERS, INC.

Published in the United States of America
by Rowman & Littlefield Publishers, Inc.
A wholly owned subsidary of The Rowman & Littlefield Publishing Group, Inc.
4501 Forbes Boulevard, Suite 200, Lanham, Maryland 20706
www.rowmanlittlefield.com

Estover Road
Plymouth PL6 7PY
United Kingdom

British Library Cataloguing in Publication Information Available

Library of Congress Cataloging-in-Publication Data

Freud at 150 : 21st-century essays on a man of genius / edited by Joseph P.
Merlino . . . [et al.].
    p. cm.
"A Jason Aronson book."
Includes bibliographical references and index.
ISBN-13: 978-0-7657-0548-8 (cloth : alk. paper)
ISBN-10: 0-7657-0548-6 (cloth : alk. paper)
ISBN-13: 978-0-7657-0547-1 (pbk. : alk. paper)
ISBN-10: 0-7657-0547-8 (pbk. : alk. paper)
    1. Freud, Sigmund, 1856–1939. 2. Psychoanalysts—Austria—Biography. 3.
Psychoanalysis. 4. Freud, Sigmund, 1856–1939. I. Merlino, Joseph P. II. Title: Freud at
one hundred fifty.
    BF109.F74F683 2008
    150.19'52092—dc22   2007019600

Printed in the United States of America

⊗™ The paper used in this publication meets the minimum requirements of American
National Standard for Information Sciences—Permanence of Paper for Printed Library
Materials, ANSI/NISO Z39.48-1992.

Contents

Preface

In his correspondence with Albert Einstein, Sigmund Freud wrote the famous line: "Whatever makes for cultural development is working also against war." The letter dates from 1932, a time of political, social, and economic instability in Europe following the devastation of World War I, and with the even bigger catastrophes of National Socialism, World War II, and the Holocaust looming on the horizon. It was certainly not a good time for optimistic beliefs in the power of culture to change the world. Freud himself was far from being that naïve; after all, wasn't he the one who shattered the belief in human nature's inherent morality and found humans capable of the worst, unrestrained by rational, ethical, or cultural barriers? It would have been desirable for humanity if Freud had been wrong. However, the atrocities of the National Socialist regime proved him correct beyond the worst assumptions.

Why did Freud still advocate cultural development as a remedy to violent conflicts? Maybe another important quote by Freud clarifies this point: "The voice of the intellect is a soft one but it does not rest till it has gained a hearing." Despite all appropriate pessimism, despite all frustrating experiences, there is no viable alternative to cultural development for the sustainable promotion of the "voice of the intellect." While even convinced pacifists agree that in extreme cases violence may be needed to end violence, as was the case in World War II, even military hardliners agree that any successful settlement of an armed conflict has to be accompanied by a perspective for human and cultural development. This is the only way to break the vicious circle of violence triggering more violence.

Freud's insights have lost none of their significance for our present time, as was pointed out in many events organized in Austria and abroad in 2006 to honor the 150th anniversary of Freud's birth. I was particularly intrigued by the symposium "Freud's Place in our Minds: A Day of Reflection on Sigmund Freud's Significance in the 21st Century," the contribution to the Freud celebrations by the four major U.S. psychoanalytic organizations: The American Academy of Psychoanalysis and Dynamic Psychiatry; The American Psychoanalytic Association; The American Psychological Association, Division 39 (Psychoanalysis); and The National Membership Committee for Psychoanalysis in Clinical Social Work. The symposium was organized in cooperation with and hosted by the Embassy of Austria in Washington, D.C. It is very gratifying that the excellent presentations have been published. I hope that this book will be inspiring for many readers as an effort to make "the voice of the intellect" heard.

Heinz Fischer
Federal President of the Republic of Austria

Acknowledgments

The Psychoanalytic Consortium is a coalition of four major psychoanalytic membership organizations in the United States: The American Academy of Psychoanalysis and Dynamic Psychiatry; The American Psychoanalytic Association; The Division of Psychoanalysis (39) of the American Psychological Association; and The National Membership Committee for Psychoanalysis in Clinical Social Work. These four organizations represent psychoanalysts in the core mental health professions of clinical social work, psychiatry, and psychology.

The consortium member organizations first joined together in 1992 to promote the advancement of psychoanalysis and to ensure the highest standards of training and practice of psychoanalysis in the United States. The concerns of the consortium have included: advisement on mental health matters; protection of the public interest in ensuring the right to seek psychoanalytic treatment; education of the public about the value of psychoanalytic therapy; and promotion of collaborative scientific and educational endeavors. Notable achievements of the consortium have been the ratification of the Standards of Psychoanalytic Education (2001) and the subsequent facilitation of the formation of the Accreditation Council for Psychoanalytic Education (2003), the entity charged with the evaluation and the accreditation of psychoanalytic training programs in the United States.

Through its work, the consortium has expanded and enriched American psychoanalysis in many ways. Furthermore, the alliance has proven to be a rewarding collaboration for each of the member organizations, which has benefited from the rich diversity, ongoing exchange of ideas, and mutual support fostered by the affiliation.

To commemorate the 150th anniversary of the birth of Sigmund Freud, the founder of psychoanalysis, the Embassy of Austria in Washington, D.C., invited the four member organizations of the consortium to plan a symposium in honor of the contributions of Sigmund Freud to contemporary culture and society. This event became a reality with the program, *Freud's Place in Our Minds: A Day of Reflection on Sigmund Freud's Significance in the 21st Century.*

On September 15, 2006, this historic gathering took place at the Austrian Embassy in Washington, D.C. It was an exciting day for the diverse group of psychoanalysts assembled. Differences in theory and practice were outweighed by the many commonalities of thought. The participants experienced a unique scholarly exchange in an atmosphere of openness and cooperation. This has inspired the publication of these symposium proceedings together with a collection of thought-provoking essays and historic photographs prepared to mark this anniversary of Freud's birth.

The result is this present work, *Freud at 150: 21st-Century Essays on a Man of Genius.* The Psychoanalytic Consortium members are greatly indebted to the vision and efforts of H. E. Eva Nowotny, Ambassador of Austria to the United States, and to Ms. Margareta Ploder, Director Austrian Cultural Forum Embassy of Austria, as well as their staff, to whom we extend heartfelt appreciation for their commitment to psychoanalysis.

Many of the chapters contained herein appear in published form for the first time. The editors gratefully acknowledge permission to reprint the other chapters as follows:

Chapter 1, "Sigmund Freud: Conquistador of the Unconscious," was originally published in 2006 by the Austrian Federal Ministry for Foreign Affairs. Reprinted with permission.

Chapter 2, "Is Psychoanalysis an Art, a Science, a Religion, or a Fraud," was originally published in 2006 by the Austrian Federal Ministry for Foreign Affairs. Reprinted with permission.

Chapters 3 through 9, "Die Enthüllung des 21. Jahrhunderts," were originally published in 2006 by the Austrian Libraries and Cultural Forums. Reprinted with permission.

Part 2 of chapter 13, "Psychoanalysis and Society: Can Psychoanalysis Help to Understand Modern Conflicts? A Social Worker Speaks," was originally published in *News & Views* (December 2006), newsletter of the Greater Washington Society for Clinical Social Work. Reprinted with permission.

Introduction

Eva Nowotny, Austrian Ambassador to the United States

On September 15, 2006, I had the pleasure of hosting the Symposium *"Freud's Place in our Minds: A Day of Reflection on Sigmund Freud's Significance in the 21st Century"* at the Austrian Embassy in Washington, D.C. This symposium was organized in cooperation with The American Academy of Psychoanalysis and Dynamic Psychiatry, The American Psychoanalytic Association, The American Psychological Association, Division 39 (Psychoanalysis), and The National Membership Committee for Psychoanalysis in Clinical Social Work and was the highlight of the Embassy's many events in honor of Sigmund Freud's 150th birthday.

The presentations and discussions were extraordinarily stimulating, and many participants felt that those thoughts ought to be shared with a wider audience. This vision has become a reality with the book that you hold in your hands. I would like to express my sincerest gratitude to the four organizations for having made this publication possible, to all participants for their contributions, to Edith Kurzweil for contributing her essay "Sigmund Freud: Conquistador of the Unconscious," which was first published by the Austrian Ministry for Foreign Affairs, and to Multiart, an agency coordinating the activities for the Freud Year 2006 on behalf of the Austrian Foreign Ministry, for including the materials of the Freud exhibition "Unveiling the 21st Century."

Much has changed since Freud's publication of "The Interpretation of Dreams" on January 1, 1900, a date deliberately chosen for its significance, heralding a new century and a new worldview and in popular opinion considered the date of birth of psychoanalysis. Freud's findings, without any doubt, did change the world and the way we look at ourselves, at each other, and at society. On the other hand, the further course of history did not leave psychoanalysis unaffected either. Many aspects of Freud's legacy were challenged as evidenced by the question featured on the front page of *Time* magazine in 1993: "Is Freud Dead?"

Some of Freud's beliefs may have passed away along with him. But was psychoanalysis only an episode in history, and have we now gone back to a pre-Freudian world? Is "the plague" he brought us extinct? Or is Eric Kandel, neurobiologist and Medicine Nobel Laureate 2000, right, when he suggested not long ago that "psychoanalysis still represents the most coherent and intellectually satisfying view of the mind"?

Probably, going back to a time "before Freud" is as unimaginable as going back to "before Newton." Freud gave us the keys to a new dimension in the rational and scientific understanding of human beings, including when they act in the most irrational way. These keys have evolved and have been refined but we keep using them. Obviously, new insights complemented and partly supplanted those of Freud. Of course, some of his findings were determined by the society in which he lived. But so far no alternative has emerged to convincingly challenge the set of understandings that we were given by Freud: namely, that each individual has an inner world; that the—often repressed— unconscious affects our well-being and our relations with others; that our psyches are not whole but are divided into parts that are usually in conflict with each other; that humans tend toward certain forms of motivated irrationality of which they have little or no awareness; and that many of these insights also apply to culture, society, and politics.

It is one of the tragic ironies in history that Freud's unsettling findings about human nature and group behavior could immediately be verified in political practice when Nazism was thrusting Europe into its biggest catastrophe. Seemingly rational citizens turned on their fellow citizens and committed or condoned atrocities that shook the belief in the power of culture and civilization forever. Freud and his family were forced to flee from the city where he had spent seventy-eight years of his life; Freud's sisters who stayed in Vienna were murdered in the Holocaust.

However, Freud also showed ways and means of engaging in a healing process, both individually and collectively. A crucial part of this healing is making efforts to face the truth through remembrance and the recollection of repressed memories.

Freud's insights were relevant for the political circumstances surrounding their creation. They are still relevant today when once again we have to deal with fundamentalist threats.

I hope that this book will stimulate further and critical discussion on *Sigmund Freud's Significance in the Twenty-first Century*.

1

SIGMUND FREUD

Conquistador of the Unconscious

Freud with Father
Courtesy of Multiart.

1

Sigmund Freud

Conquistador of the Unconscious

Edith Kurzweil

What might our world be like if Freud had not discovered the dynamics of the unconscious? If he had not, as he stated, "agitated the sleep of mankind," would we still be in the dark about the causes of psychosomatic disorders? Would we believe that "hysterical patients suffer from reminiscences, [whose] . . . symptoms are residues of particular (traumatic) experiences;"[1] or that our rational and independent selves are subject to internal and conflicting impulses? Would we still be using the doctor's gaze and hypnosis to uncover unconscious motivations, or assume that our moods are controlled by "humours?" And might poets alone have access to our unconscious?

Obviously we have no answers to such enigmatic questions. But as it is, we cannot ignore the fact that it was Freud who took leave of neurology and arrived at psychoanalysis. Nor can we ignore the fact that the early practitioners of psychoanalytic therapy formed a movement and, however haphazardly, intentionally or unintentionally, spread therapeutic thinking throughout modern culture. By now Freud's concepts are part of our daily lives: we make "Freudian slips"; we compensate, feel guilty, and interpret dreams; we deny reality, have Oedipal wishes and oral or anal compulsions; we suffer from trauma and may be narcissistic, masochistic or sadistic—without recalling that Freud coined these idioms—or that our criminal and welfare systems are drenched in regulations that rely on the theories he proposed.

WHO WAS FREUD?

Sigmund Freud was born 150 years ago, on May 6, 1856, in the small town of Freiberg (Pribor) in Moravia. His father, Jacob Freud, was a wool merchant,

Freud and Martha Bernays at Their Engagement, 1882
Courtesy of Multiart.

who, when Freud was four years old, after a short stay in Leipzig, moved his family to Vienna. His mother, Amalia Nathanson, was Jacob's much younger third wife. He had two half-brothers, one of whose sons was a year older than his uncle, Sigmund.

After the Freuds settled in Vienna, Sigmund's four younger sisters and his brother, Alexander, were born in rapid succession. Clearly, it was a lively household; in the midst of complex family ties and relations, Freud was his mother's "golden Sigi." His father often was in financial straights, as were most immigrant Jewish families, especially before emancipation in 1867. And anti-Semitism was rampant. Freud recalled that when he was ten or twelve years old, he asked his father about it. To illustrate that the Jews' lot had improved, Jacob told him of an incident in Galicia when a gentile who had come toward him on the street had knocked his hat into the gutter. "What did you do?" Sigmund asked his father. "I stepped into the gutter and picked up my cap," Jacob replied. Freud remembered that he then had compared his father unfavorably to Hannibal's father, who had made his son swear that he would take revenge on the Romans.[2]

By the time Freud attended Vienna's Sperlgymnasium, he was an avid reader and a stellar student. He became fluent in Greek, Latin, French, and English. He immersed himself in Greek philosophy and ancient history. He read Schopenhauer and Nietzsche, Goethe and Schiller, Shakespeare and Dostoevsky, and so on. After graduating, in 1873, he enrolled in the law faculty of the University of Vienna but soon switched to medicine. He also took every opportunity he could to travel—thereby broadening his horizon. Thus he managed to visit his half-brothers in Manchester and to fulfil his dream of seeing Rome and its ancient treasures. After he had received a grant for research on the gonads of eels, he spent a semester in Trieste's Zoological Experimental Station.

Upon his return to Vienna, Freud linked up with Ernst Brücke, the celebrated German physiologist—whom he later would recall as the most important of his teachers. During his year out for compulsory military service, Freud translated four essays by John Stuart Mill into German. But then he returned to Brücke's laboratory to investigate Darwin's controversial theory of evolution, on the nerve cells of crayfish; and on the psychology of human emotions. Clearly, his range of interests and achievements were exceptional.

In April 1882 Freud met, fell in love with, and became engaged to Martha Bernays, the daughter of a well-to-do Jewish family from Wandsbek, near Hamburg. Now that he planned to marry and would have to support his future family, he set aside his laboratory work and concentrated on studying for his medical degree. During the ensuing four years of separation from his fiancée, he poured his hopes and disappointments, as well as his love and devotion, into letters to Martha. Written while he was on a stipend in Paris, these communications convey his admiration for Jean-Martin Charcot, the famous neurologist and director of the asylum, Salpêtriere, who before an invited public cured hysterical patients under hypnosis, at least temporarily.

In the early 1880s Freud's older colleague and friend, Joseph Breuer, had been treating Anna O. (Bertha Pappenheim). Indeed, Breuer had uncovered the sexual components of her hysterical symptoms but was unprepared for the direction of her unconscious sexual fantasy and its elaboration into the physical contractions of a hysterical birth—a pseudocyesis—with Breuer himself as impregnator. In consternation, Breuer precipitously turned the patient over to Freud. Only years later could Freud convince the reluctant Breuer to co-publish this case.

THE BIRTH OF PSYCHOANALYSIS

Psychoanalysis came onto the world stage on January 1, 1900, with the publication of Freud's *The Interpretation of Dreams*. A year later, in *On Dreams*, Freud explained that when his scientific forays had not rendered the data he was seeking, he had found that some of his patients had helped him diagnose the cores of their neuroses. While telling him of her dreams, "Fräulein Elizabeth von R.," noticed that she recovered more forgotten material when Freud allowed her to ramble instead of questioning or hypnotizing her. Freud listened to her and adopted "free association" as his regular technique. He found that patients resisted the upsurge of repressed traumatic memories; and that physical symptoms increased when unpleasant memories came up.

At the time, philosophers perceived dreams as a peculiar state of mental functioning; medical experts tended to attribute them to an activity forced on the sleeping brain by physiological stimuli; and in popular opinion they were thought of as manifestations of demonic or divine powers, or were being explained as specific symbols—to which serious people answered that "*Träume sind Schäume*" (dreams are froth).[3] But having clued in to the pathologies of some of his patients, Freud concluded that dreams had sexual origins. To check on the veracity of this then-outlandish supposition as well as on his method of listening, he undertook a painful self-analysis: he interpreted every detail of his dreams and associated their fragments in relation to events in the distant past and to those of the preceding day.

Aware that dreams are soon forgotten, Freud would immediately write down everything he could recall. He then would reflect on this manifest dream content, segment by segment. By following the associations to each separate segment, he would eventually arrive at some understanding of its latent content. The latter, he divided into three categories: those that made sense and were intelligible; others that were bewildering; and yet others that seemed disconnected, confused, and meaningless. Ultimately, he found that decoded dreams stand revealed as wish-fulfilments—which in young children, who do not yet repress much, are undisguised. Even a longer summary could not do justice to the multifaceted analyses and insights that are contained in his voluminous *Interpretation of Dreams.*

A month after its publication, on February 1, 1900, Freud wrote to his friend and confidant, Wilhelm Fliess:

> I am actually not at all a man of science, not an observer, not an experimenter, not a thinker. I am by temperament nothing but a conquistador, an adventurer. If you want it translated—with all the curiosity, daring and tenacity characteristic of a man of this sort. Such people are customarily esteemed only if they have been successful, have really discovered something, otherwise they are dropped by the wayside. And that is not altogether unjust. At the present time, however, luck has left me.[4]

Clearly, this letter reflects the emotional letdown of a writer who has finished a difficult project—a project based on his innermost person as well as on his neurological training. The papers Freud had published about the evolutionary processes of the nervous structures of fish were links in the chain that by 1893 began to underpin his lectures, and his insight into the sexual roots of his patients' hysteria.[5] He carried these insights as far as was possible within the neuroscience of that time, in the "Project" (1895). Though unpublished in his lifetime, the "Project" has been considered the "Rosetta stone" that defines psychoanalysis as a natural science[6]—at least by classical psychoanalysts.

INITIAL FORAYS

Freud recovered from what he later referred to as his "splendid isolation" by the time he had acquired a handful of disciples. Toward the end of 1902, on Wednesday evenings, Alfred Adler, Otto Rank, Wilhelm Stekel, Max Kahane, and Rudolf Reitler, began to congregate in Freud's apartment at Berggasse 19. Together they investigated how, and in what way neurotic behavior might be eliminated, or at least attenuated. They brought in their dreams and associated to them, analyzed each other as well as disturbed individuals, literary classics, and their creators. In the process, they perfected—and disagreed on—the most effective clinical techniques and methods to penetrate into, and to unravel, human motives.

By October 1906 these Wednesday evenings had drawn others—mostly writers and educators, physicians, and progressive thinkers. From Rank's record of the proceedings, we learn that they were an enthusiastic bunch and had high hopes for doing away with individuals' neuroses and for liberalizing their society. To these ends, they analyzed patients, scrutinized literary masterpieces, and argued about both psychoanalytic methods and diagnoses. That was when Freud found, for instance, that "psychoanalytic abstinence"— avoiding relations with patients who were of social, business, loving, or hostile relations—allowed the psychoanalyst to lead the way in an "uncontaminated field; and that transference—that subtle and shifting relation between patient and therapist—was a tool best utilized by using close observation, correct interpretation and free association. (After recognizing that his own responses and reactions were as important as those of his patients, Freud began to conceptualize the role of the "counter-transference.")

Clinical successes inspired ever more inquiries by doctors who expected to heal their patients via the "talking cure." Freud was pleased every time he received a letter from a philosopher or a theologian, a psychologist or a writer. He was especially delighted when, in January 1907, Max Eitingon from Zurich's Burghölzli clinic attended on a Wednesday evening. Eitingon remarked on the lively and contentious spirit among these Viennese pioneers. And, when six weeks later his colleagues Carl Jung and Ludwig Binswanger appeared as well, Freud finally conceded that his discoveries were spreading. By then, he had published *The Psychopathology of Everyday Life* (1903), *Jokes and their Relation to the Unconscious* (1905), and *Three Essays on the Theory of Sexuality* (1905).

On these Wednesdays, designated participants introduced their most recent cases. Freud nearly always had the last word by synthesizing and summarizing, and adding judgments and advice. In fact, his fertile mind free-associated to scientific, social, and political topics while finding their deep connections to sexuality and the Oedipus complex.

For the most part, the majority of Viennese resisted his ideas because he attributed specific (traumatic) childhood experiences against a background of normal childhood sexuality. At that period of time, children allegedly were unaware of what they saw and heard (even though most of them shared their parents' bedrooms), were assumed to be devoid of sexual sensations, and thus were blind to the eroticism around them. In other words, most of Freud's contemporaries could not accept that conflicts caused by unacknowledged sexual drives and socially imposed prudery were the underpinnings of neuroses.

The medical establishment as well strongly resisted and rejected psychoanalysis. That the popular satirist, Karl Kraus, in *Die Fackel* (The Torch), dubbed it the disease whose cure it claims did not help. For how could dreams and conversations, however conscientious and systematic, be turned into science? That Freud tried to interest his medical colleagues in Charcot's hypnotic methods of treatment was yet another irritant. But his and his disciples' publications invited controversies, which, however upsetting to Freud, led more and more intellectuals to wonder about the impact of unconscious phenomena. Only gradually would some Viennese accept their sexuality more openly—as discussions of it, literally, started to move into Vienna's and then the worlds' drawing rooms. That is how Freud set the stage for twentieth century discourse as much as Marx and Darwin had set it for the end of the nineteenth century.

Still, as more and more disciples were gathering, free-associating, and elaborating on these ideas, trouble was brewing. Now that their comments and opinions were being recorded, some took to posturing; others were thinking of posterity and wanted credit for their original formulations and insights; and yet others zigzagged between exploring their own unconscious and expressing solidarity with friends within the group.

After forty-two of Freud's followers had met in Salzburg, in 1908, and the Hungarian, Sandór Ferenczi, had inspired them to set up the International Psychoanalytic Association (IPA), the Viennese also organized more formally. But tensions mushroomed. Because Freud did not want his creation to be perceived as a Jewish science, he chose to bestow the leadership of the IPA on Jung: he assumed that the Swiss contingent might be more acceptable to the rest of the world to head his movement. This upset the Viennese.

The breakthrough came in 1909 when the philosopher G. Stanley Hall invited Freud to America, to Clark University, in Massachusetts. He delivered a cohesive and upbeat presentation, his *Introductory Lectures on Psychoanalysis*, and received much acclaim. In addition to his host, the philosopher William James, the psychologist Edward Bradford Titchener, Freud's first translator A. A. Brill, the psychiatrist Adolph Meyer, the anthropologist Franz Boas, the foremost neurologist James Jackson Putnam, and even the anarchist leader Emma Goldman came to listen.

Now, Freud had achieved the fame he had sought all along; and the future of psychoanalysis was secure. But the disciples increasingly disagreed about theoretical and clinical issues. These, in turn, had political implications.

BROKEN FRIENDSHIPS AND ENSUING RIVALRIES

For some time Adler had maintained that the sources of neuroses originated in "morphological phenomena of organ deficiency," whether or not the sexual organ was involved. If that were so, one did not have to search for the deeply buried, elusive unconscious. Of course, Freud could not accept Adler's postulate, or the centrality of aggressive drives. After much discord, Adler, along with a number of others, broke away and in 1911 started his own organization, Individualpsychologie.

Two years later Jung defected. His earlier research about *dementia praecox* had led him to diagnose his patients' regressions as past fixations due to difficulties in the present, rather than to their inability to free themselves of early trauma. And unlike Freud, who attributed unacceptable dreams to indirect expressions of wishes, Jung's long-standing interest in comparative religion and mythology "led him to detect parallels with psychotic material . . . common to all men."[7] His was a collective unconscious rather than a personal one, whereas Adler's system was "founded entirely on the impulse of aggression." At least that was Freud's verdict in his *History of the Psycho-Analytic Movement*.[8]

Freud held firm. He insisted that neither spiritual nor social issues were to shunt the unconscious, the "gold of psychoanalysis," to the sidelines. So he concentrated even more on the transference as the tool that would allow the patient's infantile trauma to surface and that relied on the psychoanalyst's authenticity, honesty, and confidentiality—on his counter-transference. (Inevitably, such a subjective and private relationship cannot be controlled or judged by outsiders; and it was [and continues] being revised and refined in line with increasing insights as well as with shifting beliefs and clinical advances.)

After Adler split with Freud, he and his supporters, with the help of his backers in the Socialist party, managed to introduce psychoanalytic principles into Vienna's school system: teachers were taught to ameliorate their pupils' feelings of inferiority and to observe what was underpinning emotions of superiority. Thereby, they introduced progressive education. But few teachers, themselves, were analyzed. (Freud also voted for the Socialists but kept his science out of politics.) Jung's followers, for the most part, remained at the Burghölzli and pursued analytical psychology—which was rooted in the collective unconscious, in ancestral archetypes. Both of their approaches promised faster and less painful cures than Freud's search for the unconscious and thereby were more easily accepted by the public. (From then on, most psychoanalysts' disputes were settled by defections rather than discussions.)

The classical Freudians' direct contact with the general public had to wait until Karl Abraham and Max Eitingon set up their first polyclinic in 1920 in Berlin. And until August Aichhorn started to work with delinquents (wayward youths) in post World War I Vienna. Helene Deutsch soon founded the Kinderheim Baumgarten for about 300 homeless Jewish, working class orphans. In 1922 Anna Freud set up her kindergarten and a free clinic for the poor. But none of these endeavors reached as deeply into the Viennese community as did Adler's individual psychology.

At the outbreak of World War I, Freud had rooted for Austria's victory until it had suddenly occurred to him that Ernest Jones, the president of the British contingent, "belonged to the enemy." In "The Disillusionment of the War" he tried to come to grips with the fact that civilized nations so easily turn against each other with hate and loathing. And he thought that the renunciation of instinctual satisfaction might overcome this problem, if "the influence of civilization . . . [were to] transform egoistic trends into altruistic ones."[9] (A lofty goal, which we have as yet to reach.)

Two of Freud's sons were in the armed forces, as were Ferenczi and Abraham. They contributed a number of articles about war neuroses to the *Internationale Zeitschrift für Psychoanalyse*. So did a newcomer, Ernst Simmel. Freud tackled the issues by focusing on the unconscious sources of narcissism and autoeroticism, and of aggressive drives—oral, anal and phallic. In 1923 in *The Ego and the Id*, he went on to postulate three structures: id, ego, and superego.[10] Simply put, the id always remains unconscious, is present from birth, and always presses to satisfy its needs; the ego negotiates between the id's push to get what it wants and the superego; the moral demands of the superego are a sort of internalized conscience.

Nearly every subsequent theoretical innovation, including some therapies that purport to reject Freudianism, have taken issue with one or another of Freud's concepts. Until his death in September 1939, Freud, for the most part, wrote additions, addenda, or revisions of previous works. Increasingly, he focused on questions of religion and culture.

FREUD'S ENDEAVORS SURVIVE

Freud died in London after he had gone into exile, fleeing the Nazis' regime in Austria, and Hitler's armies had marched into Poland. Thanks to the quick actions of American and British members of the IPA, the lives of many Jewish psychoanalysts, though not all of them, were saved. So, by the time the IPA once again convened in Zurich in 1949, 90 percent of the members spoke English, many with a German accent. Among the 800 participants, over half were American. Indeed, by then, psychoanalysis had caught on among American intellectuals, some of whom had been analyzed by refugee psychoanalysts. A few of the immigrants had bestowed a certain amount of prestige on the profession: Walter Langer had furnished a psychological portrait of Hitler; Kurt Eissler had investigated what personality types were best suited to lead soldiers; the foremost sociologist, Talcott Parsons, had begun to collaborate with Heinz Hartmann in order to locate the innermost, unconscious links that underpin psychological and social behavior; Erich Fromm's bestseller, *The Fear of Freedom*,[11] had made applied psychoanalysis sound easy, almost a cure-all for individuals and societies. As had Karen Horney's *The Neurotic Personality of our Time*.[12]

Now, institutional struggles mushroomed. Because in the United States anyone could hang out a shingle claiming to practice psychoanalysis, the Freudians—against Freud's strong protests[13]—had set out to protect themselves by restricting membership to medical doctors. But when, after World War II, Theodor Reik, one of the Viennese pioneers, was not admitted to the New York and the American Psychoanalytic Associations, he started his own training institute for lay analysts. By then, Karen Horney and Clara Thompson had left the classical Freudians to develop a more feminist and culture-oriented approach, the Horney School; so had Sandór Rado and Abram Kardiner, to pursue more anthropological rather than ego-oriented, investigations. They had formed, respectively, the William Alanson White Institute and the Columbia University Institute for Psychoanalytic Training. More "defections" followed. Other therapeutic groupings—whether neo-Freudian or anti-Freudian—sprang up over the years, so that at the most recent count, there were around four hundred different psychotherapeutic associations in America alone. Altogether, in one way or another, all of these are Freud's descendants and are responsible for the "therapeutic society" we have come to live in. Most of the offsprings condemn the strict Freudians as retrograde. It is worth noting, however, that in accordance with the changing Zeitgeist, all branches of psychoanalysis have countenanced looser rules.

In England Anna Freud and Melanie Klein had their "Controversial Discussions" in 1943–1944, which revolved around who would control Freud's heritage—on standards of training, length of analysis, and psychoanalysis' intellectual thrust. Ultimately, they agreed to allow candidates to choose among Anna Freud's "traditional views," Melanie Klein's mother-oriented approach, and the Middle group. But they mandated that candidates acquaint themselves with the other directions. In 1984 Joseph Sandler reminisced that the Londoners "psychoanalytic taste corresponded to the training one had, but one learned to listen to others, and this allowed for eclecticism."[14] Moreover, living with divergent theories encouraged institutional flexibility as well as innovative thinking. The proliferation of therapeutic organizations alone could not have created the climate for therapy. Nor, *mutatis mutandis*, could this therapeutic milieu have cured neuroses. But because neurotic behavior was ubiquitous and more entrenched than the young Freud believed, the search for the unconscious continued. (By the end of his life Freud had become more pessimistic.) Still, many individuals had been helped, and had learned to live happier lives, even though their neuroses had not fully disappeared. Therefore, the promises for cures have continued to loom ahead, as therapists of every stripe claim success via newer and seemingly simpler and faster methods. And whereas Freud had aimed only to analyze the neuroses, his descendants and their patients have targeted every kind of psychopathology and have assumed that psychoanalysis, like the American Constitution and the Bill of Rights, assures them life, liberty and the (successful) pursuit of happiness.

Psychoanalysts and psychotherapists could not have practiced their skills without a population that expected to live ever more freely, and whose members needed to break away from parental, religious and/or social constraints. In America, in the aftermath of World War II, the G.I. Bill of Rights had opened up higher education to former members of the armed forces; to some of them the return to civil life had proven to be too difficult, so that they turned to psychoanalysts for guidance.

In Germany, the physicians Alexander and Margarete Mitscherlich went to London to get a psychoanalytic training before starting the Sigmund Freud-Institut in Frankfurt am Main, in order to help understand, and eventually liberate, their countrymen's psyches from the Nazi past. The Frankfurt School, under the guidance of Max Horkheimer and Theodor Adorno, almost assured young Germans that a fusion of Freud's and Marx's ideals would serve that same end, and would help avoid future wars, Holocausts, and murderous governmental regimes. Thus Freud's descendants searched in his texts for the therapeutic formula that would avoid the blunders of earlier periods. In Austria, this happened to a lesser extent and somewhat later. However, none of that might have occurred had there not been IPA meetings and the widespread proliferation of psychoanalytic thought by writers and cultural critics, philosophers and theologians.

PSYCHOANALYSIS AND CREATIVITY

In his letter to Wilhelm Fliess, on October 15, 1897, Freud reflected that:

> One could understand the gripping power of *Oedipus Rex* on the audience, . . .
> [because] everyone was once a budding Oedipus in fantasy and each recoils in
> horror from the dream fulfilment here transplanted into reality, with the full
> quantity of repression which separates his infantile state from his present one.[15]

Freud went on to speculate that *Hamlet's* unconscious grappled with his unconscious patricidal fantasy as well as with the real event of the father's murder by his uncle before he could avenge his father's death. And he cited other examples to show that literary composition is born in commonplace activities; that myths often inspire literary creation; and that "a strong experience usually . . . precedes a wish which finds its fulfilment in creative work."

In *Leonardo da Vinci. A Study in Psychosexuality*, (1900) Freud elaborated on the roots of creativity more fully. After covering the enormous literature about Leonardo, Freud presented him as an illegitimate child who had been deprived of a father figure until perhaps his fifth year. And after extensively analyzing Leonardo's extraordinary accomplishments—from painting and sculpture to architecture, from geology to flying—Freud conceded that he did not have enough information to connect Leonardo's psyche's primal forces to his productivity. Nevertheless, he deduced that when in his early fifties Leonardo had painted the Mona Lisa, a "deeper strata of his psychic content became active again . . . to the benefit of his art, . . . [and] awakened in him the memory of the happy and enraptured smile of his mother, and under the influence of this awakening he reacquired the stimulus which guided him in the beginning of his artistic efforts."[16] In sum, Leonardo, who was sexually inactive, had repressed sexuality but sublimated the libidinal drives into a thirst for knowledge in many areas.

In *Dostoevsky and Parricide* (1927), Freud was more precise, by distinguishing among the creative artist, the neurotic, the moralist, and the sinner. "How is one to find one's way in this bewildering complexity," Freud then asked. He answered that Dostoevsky's sinning was induced by his boundless egotism and a strong destructive tendency; and that his love of humanity infused his morality. As to his neurosis, Freud conjectured that it might well have been the cause of his "impulsive character." Was it due to his epilepsy? Or was this epilepsy, itself, a serious hysteria? Could it be related to *coitus*—which the earliest doctors likened to a "little epilepsy"? Freud then noted that the description of these seizures tells us nothing and assumed that they probably had been mild in childhood and had become full-blown only after his father was brutally murdered when Dostoevsky was eighteen years old. At that point, both his love and hatred for the father were repressed—due to Dostoevsky's particularly strong bisexual disposition: the deathlike seizures were the symptoms resulting from the conflict between the writer's identification with his father and punishment by his superego. Freud attributed Dostoevsky's gambling to fits of pathological passion—a form of "self-punishment that replaces onanistic compulsion."

Like Otto Rank,[17] Freud perceived the modern artist as fleeing from life by giving shape to his unpleasant experiences in creative endeavors—in order to reach immortality by recreating himself in an "ideologically constructed ego." Consequently, psychoanalysts find the unconscious of artists to be closer to the surface than that of ordinary neurotics, and have assumed that more could be learned from their analyses than from that of other mortals.

They demonstrated that every genuine poetical creation proceeds from more than one motive, more than one impulse, in the mind of the creative artist, and admits for more than one interpretation. Freud had declared that "before the problem of the creative artist, analysis must lay down its arms." His successors have gone on to take up these arms in such a diversity of themes and approaches, that we cannot speak of a single subject, or a single question. Countless books have dealt with a bewildering array of topics, methods, and assumptions: the creative process, the relation of literature to psychoanalytic theory, the links between writers' neuroses and their work, the neurotic elements of writers' lives, the connection between literature and health, the psychic content of specific works, and the parallels between popular myths and unconscious motives. There is no unified theory. But, like Freud, no one ever was able to prove a connection between an artist's actual work and his neurotic disposition. Nor did Freud's followers share definitions or common assumptions. Among the most-cited contributions were Marie Bonaparte's *Poe and the Function of Literature*, Phyllis Greenacre's *Jonathan Swift*, Selma Freiberg's *Kafka and the Dream*, Ernst Kris's *The Contributions and Limitations of Literature*, Ernest Jones's *The Death of Hamlet's Father*, and Erich Fromm's *Franz Kafka*. Their focus on the neurotic elements of creative figures added remarkable insights into the lives and works of their subjects but did not explain the relationship between these and their impact on the work as a whole, or on what distinguished it as a superior work of art. And because in the creative process imagination plays games with observed reality, it is not easy to find the dividing line between the so-called objective world and the subjective world of the poet or the painter. Psychoanalysts' discussions of art still give a bow to Freud, although they rarely build on colleagues' contributions. On the other hand, the news media and art historians discuss the psychological world of twentieth century artists, whether focusing on Jackson Pollock and Andy Warhol, or on Louise Nevelson, by taking Freudian tenets for granted, and tend not to mention Freud or psychoanalysis.

Among the literary critics who weighed in, Erich Heller argued that the world had been ready for Freud long before he arrived, and that he had become part of the Zeitgeist—for instance, in Thomas Mann's *Death in Venice*, where Aschenbach, after having decided to leave the city, manages to lose his suitcase and must stay on; or in *The Magic Mountain*, where Hans Castorp employs his minor illness to postpone leaving the sanatorium for seven years. Goethe's *geprägte Form*, noted Heller, has been replaced with stream-of-consciousness novels and other experimental works that bear Freud's imprint. ("Literary Approaches and Theories," in *Literature and Psychoanalysis*, ed. Edith Kurzweil and William Phillips [Columbia University Press, 1983], p. 67.)

The philosopher William Barrett focused on the writer's existence, tracing the search for truth from Hegel through Marx and Freud. Only *authentic*

writers are able to find truth via their fantasies. Barrett found that when an individual is teetering on the borderline between fantasy and insanity, external
pressures often tip the balance to the side of insanity. Lionel Trilling, in *Art
and Neurosis*, leaned toward the healthy side of Barrett's equation. Myths
about poets as *genus irritable* live on, he argued, because they serve to separate poets from the Philistines. This does not mean that neurosis fuels the
artist's irreducible gift: his genius resides in his perception, realization, and
representation. William Phillips maintained that neither Barrett's nor
Trilling's theses can be proven either clinically or theoretically, and that in the
end it tends to come down to persuasion or even to common sense.[18]

These issues have not been resolved. Actually, with the advent of structuralism and deconstruction, poststructuralism, and postmodernism, the post-
Freudian tower of Babel has mushroomed and thereby has furthered many an
academic's career.

NOTES

1. S. Freud, *SE, XI*, 16.
2. Edith Kurzweil, *The Freudians. A Comparative Perspective*. Yale University
Press, 1989, p. 16.
3. S. Freud, *SE, V*, 634.
4. Letter to Wilhelm Fliess, February 1, 1900.
5. S. Freud, *SE, III*, 27.
6. Edward Erwin, ed. *The Freud Encyclopedia*. Routledge, p. 426.
7. Anthony Storr, *The Essential Jung*. Princeton: Princeton University Press, pp.
15–16.
8. S. Freud, *SE*, 14, 3.
9. S. Freud, *SE*, 14, 282. This theme occurs many times and is elaborated on in
Civilization and its Discontents.
10. S. Freud, *SE*, 19, 3.
11. Erich Fromm. *The Fear of Freedom*. London: Routledge and Keagan Paul,
1942.
12. Karen Horney. *The Neurotic Personality of Our Time*. New York: Norton.
13. S. Freud. "The Question of Lay Analysis." *SE* 20, 179.
14. Kurzweil, p. 203.
15. Jeffrey Moussaieff Masson. *The Complete Letters of Sigmund Freud to Wilhelm Fliess*. Harvard University Press, 1985, p. 172.
16. S. Freud, *SE, 11*, 134.
17. Otto Rank. *"The Artist" Der Künstler: Ans Unsätzer einer Sexual-Psycholo-
gie.*Vienna: Hugo Heller & Cie, 1907.
18. Edith Kurzweil and William Phillips, eds. *Literature and Psychoanalysis*. New
York: Columbia University Press, 1984.

2

Is Psychoanalysis an Art, a Science, a Religion, or a Fraud?

Edith Kurzweil

In 1958 the philosopher Sidney Hook organized a conference that brought together the foremost psychoanalysts and philosophers to examine the scientific value of Freud's work. They all paid homage to his genius, but doubted the existence of the unconscious. Neither of the prominent defenders of psychoanalysis—Heinz Hartmann and Lawrence Kubie—could convince these philosophers that a theory or doctrine that is determined by psychological processes may validate its scientific truth. The behaviorist John B. Watson, not surprisingly, compared the scientific worth of Freud's unconscious to the miracles of Jesus; and Adolf Grünbaum declared it half-baked because it ultimately cannot be falsified. The rest of this assembly of serious thinkers weighed in on their side. They ended up agreeing that the proportion of recoveries or improvements among neurotics who have not received psychoanalytic treatments was as great as among those who have.[1]

The mere fact that this conference was held demonstrated that psychoanalytic thought had penetrated every stratum of culture and that, as Freud had predicted, he had "brought on the plague." But intellectuals who had hoped that the proper fusion of the unconscious with Marx's humanism, such as Herbert Marcuse's *Eros and Civilization* (1955),[2] began to have doubts. Some continued promoting its radical potential, but resistance to Freud's principles was increasing.

Consequently, classical psychoanalysts went back to focus on clinical research and to generalize, albeit often too freely, from their work with patients.

By then, their movement had become truly international. IPA membership had grown, and members presented papers at more and more meetings around the globe. The center shifted away from North America, if only because elsewhere, new questions and issues arose—And new enthusiasms.

Freud Working on Manuscript of Moses & Monotheism, *1938*
Courtesy of Multiart.

IS FREUD A GODLESS JEW?

Religion was the most troubling and paradoxical problem that Freud faced and never could resolve. Already in 1907,[3] he had maintained that obsessive actions or ceremonials and the psychological processes of religious life, intrinsically, have the same origins—the sense of guilt of neurotics or the pious observances of believers. The former were the counterparts to the latter—although "in neurosis the origin is sexual and in religion springs from egoistic sources."[4]

No wonder Freud has been judged an atheist, an agnostic, and a godless Jew. In my view, his sense of religion responded to the anti-Semitism around him as well as to the phase of his theoretical inquiries at specific moments. In *Totem and Taboo* (1912–1913), he argued that taboos are more primitive phenomena than religious and moral prohibitions, but that the traces they leave behind indicate that the origins of their rituals are located in the incest taboo, in the need for tribes to survive by forbidding incestuous relations, and to do so by furthering exogamy.

The Future of an Illusion (1927), was influenced by Freud's discussions of these issues with his friend, the Swiss, Lutheran pastor, Oscar Pfister. Already in 1909, Freud had found him "a charming fellow who has won all our hearts, a warmhearted enthusiast, half Savior, half Pied Piper,"[5] who frolicked with the children and, who preferred being an "analysis-pastor" to healing spiritual misery. In their letters as well as in this publication, Freud held that the human mind had developed since the earliest times, that there had been mental advances, and that eternal coercion had become internalized—into man's superego.[6] Its cultural equivalents, he noted, are moral demands that are expressed through religion. Thus God is cast in the role of the all-powerful, protective father—the adult's equivalent of the child's father—who will severely punish any infringement of his commands. And he concluded that thereby religion "is comparable to a childhood neurosis" which civilization eventually will surmount.[7] Contrary to reason, it is the illusion of believers. Of course, Pfister disagreed; for him religion and psychoanalysis were mutually supportive, because both were looking for truth; and because theologians as well as psychoanalysts were pursuing noble human goals and strivings.

As we know, with Hitler's ascent as German chancellor in 1933, religion became an immediate and tangible issue. (By then Freud was very ill and soon after the Austrian Anschluss was allowed to flee to London.) In 1934, he had set out to write *Moses and Monotheism* (1939),[8] as a novel. He placed the murder of Moses at the roots of the worship of Yahweh. He now depicted Moses as an aristocratic Egyptian who had imposed the worship of his own deity, Aten, as the single god on the Jewish people. Because the Jews could not tolerate such a restrictive belief, they were said to have killed the tyrannical young pharaoh, but when they needed a single god to unite them had revived monotheism by worshipping Yahweh. To Freud, killing the oppressive pharaoh then paralleled the killing of the original father and the guilt of the murderous sons—as he had maintained in *Totem and Taboo* (1913) and in *Civilization and Its Discontents* (1930).

Was Freud now figuring out how to explain the Jews' flight from Egypt by means of the Oedipus complex, or was he drawing parallels with his and his coreligionists' expulsion first from Germany and then from Austria? For however assimilated Viennese Jews had been, they all had experienced anti-Semitism—even while burying their heads in the sand. Freud loved Vienna. Even as he had been aghast when his books were being burned in Germany, he had been certain that his Austrians never could behave as outrageously. In that, he was part of his Jewish milieu. After all, the Austrians' anti-Semitism had been more subtle, more subterranean than that of the Germans. Had he analyzed himself at that point, he might have found that he was in denial. This is not to say that Freud might have foreseen the favorable reception that Hitler would be given in Austria. Still, was this denial a necessary defense mechanism? A miscalculation of the political situation? Or a consequence of assimilation? Even Freud had no answer.

JACQUES LACAN'S RISE AFTER WORD WAR II

After the defeat of Hitler, just a few handfuls of psychoanalysts had remained in Austria and Germany, and their credentials were questioned. Could they have practiced under the Nazis without compromising themselves? And if that had been possible, could they have benefited from the scientific advances made elsewhere?

Or had they adapted to the regime? In the Soviet Union and its satellites, psychoanalysis had been outlawed. In the Latin American countries where European psychoanalysts had settled—Chile, Argentina, Brazil—local associations had been formed and vetted, sooner or later, by the IPA. There too, relationships by psychoanalysts with members of repressive regimes were being held up to the light. Now, investigating commissions appointed by the IPA were checking into institutional and members' pasts, and into their practices.

The French situation was unique and most consequential: Freud's teachings were kept alive by two major factions: those who accepted what by then was called "American ego psychology" and by those who were paying attention to Jacques Lacan's dissident voice. Ever since the IPA congress in Marienbad in 1936, Lacan had maintained that a child's first reflection of itself in a mirror, sometime in its second year, rather than Freud's Oedipus complex, determined its future personality. By 1949 he scandalized his peers in the *Société Psychanalytique de Paris* (SPP) by opposing their training requirements and by arguing for fewer and shorter sessions. After it had transpired that he was "supervising" over thirty candidates in addition to seeing countless patients, he was ousted from the SPP. But his reconceptualization of the Freudian unconscious as interconnected representations that subjectively structure the "symbolic order" had already attracted listeners to his public lectures before he formed his own psychoanalytic society, the *Société Française de Paris*. As did his "three registers" (the Real, the Symbolic, and the Imaginary) and his anti-American slogans—at a time when anti-Americanism was at a peak, and was fueled by Sartre's existentialism and pro-Soviet stance. Basically, Lacan parsed Freud's language and texts in line with Saussurean linguistics, employing what to the uninitiated amounted to a theoretical hocus-pocus of *signifieds* and *signifiers*. But his charismatic stage personality fascinated Parisian intellectuals and would-be intellectuals alike—whether or not they understood what he was saying.

The members of the *Société Psychanalytique de Paris* responded by refining their own take on Freud. Just like their British colleagues, a number among them increasingly questioned some of the Americans' ego psychology that dominated IPA thinking. Inevitably, they paid special attention to Freud's words, which they had to do when replying to Lacan.

By the 1970s Lacan's Freud was discussed by tout-Paris. Structuralism was in, and Lacan was one of its stars. (Roland Barthes, Michel Foucault, Claude Lévi-Strauss, and Louis Althusser were the others.) To denounce the classical Freudians, Lacan criticized their reliance on the unconscious, the transference, repetition, and the drive.[9] He did not really destroy these ideas but mocked them "in the name of the father." And he "reread" Freud's texts by deconstructing them. During nine years of public seminars, he free-associated and pondered, in his learned and idiosyncratic philosophical manner, to personalities and politics, to Mao and revolution, and to whatever came to his— occasionally trance-like—state of mind. Parisians went to hear Lacan, I repeatedly was told, because it was the best show in town. Books on psychoanalysis abounded. Public conversations and confrontations multiplied, and "rereading Freud" had become an imperative.

Lacan's ideas, however incomprehensible, were tailor-made for American universities' radical feminists. In 1980, they introduced the provocative prose by, for instance, Catherine Clément, Hélene Cixous, Luce Irigaray, and Julia Kristeva. By then, these disciples had gotten tired of Lacan. Julia Kristeva became a classical Freudian. Along with the others, she also turned to writing fiction.

In America, structuralism, and subsequently deconstruction, poststructuralism and postmodernism gained ground—at first in American universities' departments of English and then in the rest of the humanities and the social sciences. Given these "isms" and their highbrow language, their proponents seemed to glory in this obscure discourse, which set them apart from the clear-speaking colleagues who were stuck in, or preferred, old-fashioned modernism. This confluence of psychoanalytically based French innovations, feminism, *leftisant* postures, and radicalism, was well received in most American universities, although some "old-fashioned" literary critics continued to work with ego-psychological views and to explore creativity by means of Freudian categories. But as feminists, they tended to disavow Freud—blaming him for male chauvinism, patriarchy, elitism, penis envy, phallocentrism, biological determinism, and homophobia

Freud never made up his mind about homosexuality, although he theorized about instincts and object choice. He conceived it as "the original basis from which as a result of restrictions in one direction or the other, both normal and inverted types develop."[10] In his "Letter to an American Mother" in 1935, he noted that homosexuality is neither a vice nor an illness; another time, he declared that it is not a sufficient reason to exclude a potential candidate from becoming a psychoanalyst. But now, one hundred years later, in our confrontational and much more permissive climate, Freud's tentative answers are being dismissed. That he was not in the forefront of gay liberation—or for that matter of women, children, and all other oppressed groups—is being held against him, and it is forgotten that without psychoanalysis these movements might not have developed or might have done so very differently. In the interim, psychotherapists have been in the forefront as defenders of victims of abuse, of criminals, of sex offenders, and so on. Altogether, they have kept Freud's thinking alive, even as more and more critics have celebrated its death.

WHY ARE FREUD'S IDEAS STILL VALID TODAY?

When Freud abandoned his scientific "Project of 1895," he—partly—did so because he did not have the technical means to pinpoint just where specific emotions were located in the brain. He stated that, topographically, he could not localize the unconscious process in the subcortical parts of the brain. "There is a hiatus here, which at present cannot be filled, nor is it one of the tasks of psychology to fill it. Our psychical topology has *for the present* nothing to do with anatomy.[11] (Emphasis in original.)

This did not mean that Freud abandoned a neurological explanation for psychoanalysis, but that neurological and physiological understanding could not yet be brought together, and that he expected to "find a point of contact with biology,"[12] when neurology itself had evolved from thinking in terms of functions and centers to a more dynamic analysis of functional systems within the brain. Over fifty years later A. R. Luria, who early on had been taken with psychoanalysis, published *Traumatic Aphasia* in the Soviet Union. However, mostly due to the Cold War, Luria's research was not followed up in the West. Moreover, by then, neuroscience and psychoanalysis had not only gone their own way but had become competing disciplines.

In his research on brain damage, Mark Solms—using the newest technology, mostly brain imaging—found that some neurological and neuropsychological syndromes might be compatible with psychoanalytic or meta-psychological concepts. For the last twelve years, he has lectured around the world and has led a seminar at the New York Psychoanalytic Association, where neurologists have presented relevant research to psychoanalysts. Mostly, Solms has been subjecting patients with brain damage to both detailed neuropsychological examinations and psychoanalysis. Via the transference, he creates the condition for the patient's spontaneity while looking at the patient's brain's functional anatomy and metabolism and pinpoints the exact areas of the brain that correspond to specific moods and emotions.

This does not mean that the riddle of the unconscious, or even of the conscious, has as yet been solved, but only that this type of research may get a bit closer to an understanding of the mind/body problems. Psychoanalysts, I believe, have everything to gain from such collaborations, and not only because it reinforces their scientific credentials in the eyes of critics. This does not mean that they ever again will get many patients to undergo four or five hours per week of treatment. However, psychoanalysts are equipped to pursue the clinical research that none of the short-term therapists are able to undertake.

Still, Freudian therapy has lost its cachet, also, because psychiatrists have been prescribing Prozac and other antidepressants as quicker fixes. According to Algis Valiunas:

> These days, psychiatrists tend to treat mental illness as principally an affliction not of the mind but of the brain—a condition, that is marked by a deficiency or excess of certain neurochemicals, which medication can restore to healthy levels. The pill has replaced the couch as the therapeutic instrument of first resort.[13]

Although Valiunas is dubious that neurochemicals ever will become the means to a free moral life, their availability is attuned to our post-modern and self-indulgent culture. The extent of this freedom was evident from the report about "Psychotherapy on the Road to . . . Where?",[14] that described the get-together, in California, of 9,000 psychologists, social workers, and students, along with many of the world's most celebrated living therapists. Some participants compared this conference to a rock concert and to a 1960s war protest. Others recalled the 1960s and 1970s "characters like Carl Rogers, Minuchin, Frankl . . . and Milton Erickson." These had been just a few of the many mind-healers who then were promoting their own abbreviated treatments. Among the approximately four hundred existing psychoanalytic groups, objects relations, interrelational and interpersonal therapies, much like the classical Freudians, expect to reach the unconscious; the majority, however, such as encounter groups, support groups, primal therapy, transactional, subjective, interactive and cognitive therapies, as well as self-psychology, and behavioral remedies, focus on the conscious lives of their patients.

This time one of the California participants wondered whether cognitive therapy can teach thought management; another asked whether "the zeit is really geisting;" and yet another questioned whether savoring pleasure and nurturing native strengths, or wiring the brain, might "foster the integration of its disparate parts."[15] I am sure that Freud would shiver in his grave if he could, were he to know to what ends his descendants are putting his oeuvre. Of course, he did state that:

> Biology is truly a land of unlimited possibilities. We may expect it to give us the most surprising information and we cannot guess what answers it will return in a few dozen years. . . . They may be of a kind which will blow away the whole of our artificial structure of hypotheses.[16]

Undoubtedly, our culture has blown psychoanalysis into the stratosphere. But research remains earthbound. Even though, as Solms reminds us, clinical psychoanalysts are ill-equipped to re-join with neuroscience, and neuroscientists do not respect psychoanalytic knowledge, both disciplines are following in Freud's footsteps. He reminds us also that in the beginning the isolation of psychoanalysis was a necessary strategy. By now that is no longer true.

What is to be done now that Freud's ideas have become ubiquitous, that his movement has spawned myriads of psychological therapies—and reaches into biology, physiology, and neurology. Are we in a land of unlimited possibilities? What reliable information will we be gleaning from the treatment of neuroses with as yet to be discovered brain research, and from serotonin related drugs? Are these prescribed too routinely, or will they be most effective when used together with Freudian psychoanalysis?

In one way or another, treatments promising ever more happiness to individuals in all walks of life are popular, even though no clinical method as yet has solved the riddle of the unconscious. But whether or not therapists are billed as Freud's heirs, modern and post-modern culture are soaked in Freud's legacy, and his movement has turned into an avalanche.

Yes, Freud did "bring us the plague," and with it the possibility of freedom from mental suffering. Still, if by some miracle we were able to expunge his ideas, would we be able to create the good world he envisioned in his youth? Or would we want to? As it is, we are bound to go on living with the invisible dimension of human motivation he opened up. For his discoveries and insights have revolutionized the thinking of the Western world.

NOTES

1. Sidney Hook, ed. *Psychoanalysis, Scientific Method, and Philosophy.* New Brunswick, NJ: Transaction Publishers, 1990, p. 220.

2. H. Marcuse. *Eros and Civilization.* Boston: Beacon Press, 1955.

3. S. Freud. *SE*, 9, 117. *Obsessive Actions and Religious Practices.*

4. S. Freud. *SE*, 9, 116–127.

5. Peter Gay. *Freud. A Life for Our Time.* New York: Norton, pp. 191–192.

6. S. Freud. *SE*, 21, 11.

7. S. Freud. *SE*, 21, 53.

8. S. Freud. *SE*, 23, 3.

9. Jacques Lacan. *The Four Fundamental Concepts of Psychoanalysis.* Paris: Éditions du Seuil, 1973.

10. S. Freud. *SE*, 7, 1145–146. 1915 addition to *Three Essays on Sexuality.*

11. S. Freud. *SE*, 14, 174–175. *The Unconscious.*

12. Mark Solms and Oliver Turnbull. *The Brain and the Inner World.* New York: Other Press, 2002, p. 298.

13. Algis Valiunas. *Commentary* 121, no. 1 (January 2006): 59.

14. *The New York Times*, December 27, 2005, F1.

15. Ibid.

16. S. Freud. *SE*, 18, 1920g; *Beyond the Pleasure Principle*, p. 60.

II

FREUD

2006

Freud, ca. 1938
Courtesy of Multiart.

3

The Historical Context

Helmut Strutzmann

1890–1900

In Vienna the last decade of the nineteenth century is marked by the growing conflict between liberals, the bourgeoisie, and the nascent Social Democratic Party. The latent anti-Semitism is growing steadily.

A new phase of modernization also begins during this period: the remunicipalization of the infrastructure, improvement of water distribution, the creation of the city's gas system, and the electrification of the street cars, among other forms of modernization. However, the gap between workers and the wealthy bourgeoisie is growing.

Groundbreaking transformations are becoming apparent in the cultural sector. The break with Classicist painting, the emergence of Art Nouveau and the Secession movement, and the architectural revolution set in motion by Adolf Loos are indications of a new worldview.

1900–1909

The shadow of war hangs over Europe. The workers movement is putting heavy pressure on the European states. The first pan-European peace movement (Bertha von Suttner) is founded. The Zionist movement, whose way was paved by Theodor Herzl in Vienna, is constituted.

After the close of the century of the steam engine, the century of electricity begins. Key discoveries and inventions, such as the x-ray, radioactivity, and mass production of automobiles and airplanes mark this century.

Freud, 1891
Courtesy of Multiart.

In Vienna the modernization of the city continues, but social conditions do not improve. The first strikes are held, and the workers movement demands a role in the decision-making process.

Art Nouveau and Secessionism make their mark on the city's architecture. The Impressionist movement spreads to Austria. Gustav Mahler is the dominant personality at the Court Opera. Arthur Schnitzler's plays are performed with success, and the literary side of the Art Nouveau movement (Jung Wien) also comes into its own.

1910–1919

World War I causes enormous losses of life in battles characterized by protracted trench warfare. The Austro-Hungarian monarchy collapses. A small Austrian state remains, which many believe is incapable of a sustained independent existence.

Austria's former crown lands become independent republics. Monarchy is abolished in Germany.

Austria becomes a republic. In Vienna the Social Democrats are the largest political party. The first Austrian president is Karl Seitz and the first chancellor is Karl Renner. The Christian Socialist party assumes governing power in 1920. Johann Schober and Ignaz Seipel serve as chancellor.

In literature and the visual arts, Expressionism wins widespread recognition as does Cubism—mirroring, as it were, a destroyed and interrupted world. In Vienna a new direction in philosophy develops within the Vienna Circle around Moritz Schlick and later around Karl Popper. The strength of the Communist party is steadily increasing. In Russia the Bolshevik revolution prevails under Vladimir Lenin and Leon Trotsky.

1920–1929

In Vienna the Social Democrats begin a program of public housing, pedagogy, and social assistance that remains unparalleled to this day: the city's major public housing projects are built, and basic social and medical services are implemented for all citizens. An exciting new turn in literature and the arts seems to be taking hold.

The world economic crisis erupts. On the legendary Black Friday in 1929 at the New York Stock Exchange, hundreds of millions of dollars in capital, as well as major corporations and banks, are wiped out within a single day. The Creditanstalt, one of Austria's largest banks, is forced to declare insolvency. In Vienna the situation has been steadily deteriorating. The Palace of Justice is burned in 1927 and there are major worker uprisings in 1928.

Revolutionary developments occur in the cultural field: the Second Viennese School, the workers' cultural movement, the pedagogical movement, New Objectivity (*Neue Sachlichkeit*), in the visual arts, the great era of Austrian literature and philosophy. Robert Musil and Ludwig Wittgenstein pursue their own psychological investigations parallel to those of Freud.

In Europe fascism begins to take hold. Hitler's *Mein Kampf* is published. In Italy Benito Mussolini takes over the government in a putsch and installs a fascist regime. Right wing dictatorships come to power in Spain and Portugal. In Germany one government crisis follows the other. In Russia the new economic plan is put in effect. Lenin prevails over Trotsky, who is banished. After Lenin's death Stalin becomes the country's most powerful political authority.

1930–1939

In Austria the political struggle between the Social Democrats and the Christian Socialists becomes more intense. Both parties form paramilitary organizations that skirmish in the streets. In 1933 Parliament "dissolves itself," and the Christian Socialist Engelbert Dollfuss takes over the government and allies himself with Benito Mussolini. The Social Democrats are banned.

In Germany Adolf Hitler is appointed chancellor, and soon thereafter democracy is no more: the dictatorship begins. In Austria, Chancellor Dollfuss is assassinated. The National Socialists begin to commit acts of terror in Austria as well.

In 1938 German troops march into Austria. Vienna becomes a part of the German Reich. Hitler is greeted by thousands of jubilant supporters.

4

An Overview of Freud's Life

Helmut Strutzmann

YOUTH, STUDIES, AND EARLY PROFESSIONAL YEARS

Freud completed his secondary schooling in Vienna at the Gymnasium in 1873 and began his medical studies the same year. In 1881 he took his doctorate and began work at the Vienna General Hospital.

During the succeeding years Freud began to devote his attention to psychical phenomena, experimented with cocaine, and went to Paris to study under Jean-Martin Charcot, a famous specialist in hysterical disorders. In the 1880s Freud and his colleague Joseph Breuer developed a "talking cure" for treating mental disorders—a predecessor of psychoanalysis.

After studying further hysterical afflictions and publishing "On Male Hysteria," Freud developed the theory that an unconscious must exist and that it must be responsible for a large part of human behavior.

In 1886 Freud married Martha Bernays. By 1895 Martha Freud had given birth to six children: Mathilde, Jean Martin, Oliver, Ernst, Sophie, and Anna. Freud had made a name for himself as a doctor and was caring for a sizeable and elite circle of patients, but his theories continued to meet with harsh rejection by traditional physicians and scientists.

FREUD IN VIENNA'S BERGGASSE

In 1891 Freud transferred his practice and residence to Berggasse 19, where he remained until his emigration to London in 1938. Here he produced his most important works and theories. In 1897 Freud formulated his first ideas regarding the Oedipus complex, focusing attention on the phenomenon of

Freud with Grandson Stephen Gabriel (Ernst Freud's Eldest Son), ca. 1916
Courtesy of Multiart.

the son's libidinous relationship to his mother and corresponding hatred of his father.

In 1899 Freud published his first major work, *The Interpretation of Dreams*, which was symbolically dated 1900. Thus began the era of psychoanalysis. Freud defined the dream as psychical activity during sleep. On the basis of dream interpretation he developed the methods and theories of psychoanalysis.

With his later formulation of the conceptual trio "id, ego, and superego," Freud created the first model of psychical functioning. He defined the urge to experience pleasure and the pleasure principle as the driving forces behind human behavior. Subsequently Freud revised his theory to include an antagonistic second basic instinct, the death drive.

The first congress of psychoanalysts was organized in 1908, and in 1910 the International Psychoanalytic Association was founded. Freud assembled around him Alfred Adler, Carl Gustav Jung, Sándor Ferenczi, and Ernest Jones, among others—some of whom would later turn away from him to form their own schools.

Freud also devoted much of his attention to cultural, literary, and artistic phenomena, making links to psychoanalysis, as he also did with religious and anthropological topics.

During the 1920s Freud published many of his key works, including *Beyond the Pleasure Principle*, *Group Psychology and the Analysis of the Ego*, *The Ego and the Id*, *The Future of an Illusion*, and *Civilization and Its Discontents*.

Following the National Socialist takeover, his writings were forbidden and burned. Freud emigrated to England in 1938 with the words: "I can most highly recommend the Gestapo to everyone."

FREUD IN EXILE IN ENGLAND

Freud journeyed—thanks to the efforts of the psychoanalyst and former patient Marie Louise Bonaparte—via Paris to London, where he acquired a house in Hampstead. He continued to practice and completed his last great work, *Moses and Monotheism*.

Freud died on 23 September 1939 in exile in England. His work was continued by his daughter, the child analyst Anna Freud. Throughout her entire life, Anna Freud felt herself to be the guardian of his legacy, also against considerable resistance and numerous attacks.

In 1971 the Sigmund Freud Museum was opened in Vienna in Freud's former apartment at Berggasse 19. In 1964 a Sigmund Freud Institute had been established in Frankfurt. In London the Freud Museum opened, with the legendary couch as the centerpiece of its collection.

Now there are psychoanalytic associations in almost every country of the world. Hundreds of publications and scientific works on Freud and the effects of his thought appear yearly. No other Austrian scientist of the twentieth century has ever stimulated a worldwide resonance comparable to that of Sigmund Freud. His work left a major mark on twentieth-century science and culture.

FREUD AND HIS DESTINY

Sigmund Freud's life was marred by human tragedies and hard turns of fate. He himself suffered for years under enormous death anxieties, which at times even made it impossible for him to work. And then there was his scientific isolation, his exclusion from the dominant guild of classical physicians and natural scientists. It was only after several attempts and at a very late date that he received a university professorship.

A number of his colleagues deserted him after major conflicts and later turned vehemently against him: Alfred Adler, Carl Gustav Jung, Otto Rank, Wilhelm Reich, Josef Breuer.

Freud's family was often hard-hit by fate: his daughter Sophie died at the age of twenty-six, and his grandson Heinerle, who had a special place in Freud's heart, died at the age of four.

Freud himself was afflicted by cancer of the jaw, and during the last fifteen years of his life he suffered great pain. He underwent thirty-three operations.

At the age of eighty-two, Freud was forced to leave National Socialist Vienna and Austria and go into exile in England. At the age of eighty-three he died in London as a result of his cancer.

5

The Development of Psychoanalysis

Helmut Strutzmann

FREE ASSOCIATION

During the early 1890s, after experimenting with hypnotism and the consciousness-expanding use of cocaine, Freud began to develop a new method of treatment, which he referred to as psychoanalysis for the first time in a lecture in 1894. To this day, "free association" remains the fundamental principle of psychoanalysis. Patients recall their memories from the subconscious without their thoughts being directed, falsified, or influenced by the analyst, as they had been in earlier therapies and methods. The setting for this practice is made up of the couch and the analyst's chair, which is positioned out of the patient's field of view. Freud himself once provided the following cursory description of the process:

> After the patient has made himself comfortable on the couch, the physician sits down unseen behind him: Please tell me what you know about yourself, he begins the first analysis session, say whatever goes through your mind. Act as though, for instance, you were a traveler sitting next to the window of a railway carriage and describing to someone inside the carriage the changing views which you see outside.

BELLEVUE OR THE REALITY OF THE DREAM

Freud's *Interpretation of Dreams* appeared in 1899/1900 and stimulated intense debates. During the preceding years Freud had conducted a self-analysis on the basis of free association.

Freud, 1929, Max Halberstadt
Courtesy of Multiart.

Freud's revolutionary discovery is that the dream represents a reality and an activity of its own, which is directly related to the dreamer's existence. Dreaming is an activity of mental life during sleep. Freud was also the first to precisely describe the techniques and mechanisms of the dream: displacement, condensation, processing of day's residues, and repressed events. In *The Interpretation of Dreams* Freud also formulated the theory of the unconscious for the first time.

THE OEDIPAL CONFLICT

The basis is the Oedipus myth. Oedipus, who solved the riddle of the Sphinx, unknowingly kills his father and takes his mother as his wife. When he discovers his error he blinds himself and is hounded by the goddesses of vengeance.

Freud sees the Oedipus complex as a central motif and phenomenon. For him the Oedipus complex arises from the child's unconscious desire for sexual contact with one parent and death wish for the other. Later it is to a large degree responsible for unconscious guilt feelings and behavior. In the individual, a fixation on the Oedipal phase results in a more strongly developed superego. This fixation also leads to a mother or father fixation that shows itself in object-choices that are reminiscent of the real parents.

THE PSYCHICAL APPARATUS

Freud's book *The Ego and the Id* was published in 1923. In it he ordered the "psychical apparatus." The psyche begins its development as an unorganized id (literally "it") from which the ego develops in its interaction with its surroundings (socialization). Lastly the superego develops out of the ego. The superego is to a certain degree a product of the parental relationship and its influence. Freud suggested the following visualization for his model: the horse (id), rider (ego), and riding master (superego).

BEYOND THE PLEASURE PRINCIPLE: EROS AND THANATOS

On numerous occasions, Sigmund Freud transformed his theories and defined them anew. When he later distanced himself from the pure Oedipal conflict, Freud advanced the theory that there are two dominant drives: the sex drive and the death drive (Eros and Thanatos).

According to Freud there are four possibilities for altering these drives: repression, sublimation, turning against the self (the self is used as the object of a drive), and reversal into the opposite. In *Beyond the Pleasure Principle* Freud provoked great consternation among his students because he renounced his original theory of the sex drive's absolute dominance.

THE JOKE

Sigmund Freud's book on jokes numbers among his most important and also his most widely read books. For Freud, the joke—and laughing—is closely connected to the unconscious. In the joke, that which is prohibited, censored, or repressed can unfold and become reality. Freud linked the technique of the joke to that of the dream and exposed parallels between the two: condensation, displacement, censorship. "A dream still remains a wish, even though it is one that has been made unrecognizable. A joke is developed play . . . Jokes seek to gain a small yield of pleasure from the mere activity, untrammeled by needs, of our mental apparatus . . . Dreams serve predominately for the avoidance of unpleasure, jokes for the attainment of pleasure; but all our mental activities converge in these two aims."

Several passages from Freud's *Jokes and Their Relation to the Unconscious* follow:

Two Jews met in the neighborhood of the bath-house.
   "Have you taken a bath?" asked one of them.
   "What?" asked the other in return, "is there one missing?"

   A gentleman entered a pastry-cook's shop and ordered a cake; but soon he brought it back and asked for a glass of liqueur instead. He drank it and began to leave without having paid. The proprietor detained him.
   "What do you want?"
   "You've not paid for the liqueur."
   "But I gave you the cake in exchange for it."
   "You didn't pay for that either."
   "But I hadn't eaten it."

   A moocher approached a wealthy baron with a request for the grant of some assistance for his journey to Ostend. The doctors, he said, had recommended him sea-bathing to restore his health. "Very well," said the rich man, "I'll give you something towards it. But must you go precisely to Ostend, which is the most expensive of all sea-bathing resorts?"—"Herr Baron," was the reproachful reply, "I consider nothing too expensive for my health."

WHY WAR?

Freud never got very involved in party politics. He followed the rise of anti-Semitism, initially latent and later manifest, in Vienna but more as a distanced observer who reflected on the phenomenon in his writings, such as the major late work *Moses and Monotheism*. In many diary entries and letters from the twenties and thirties he expressed his worries with regard to the growth of National Socialism.

The most famous of these correspondences was his exchange of letters with Albert Einstein in the thirties, which was published in Paris in 1933 for the first time. Einstein himself had selected Freud as his partner for this correspondence and opened it with the question: "Is there any way of delivering mankind from the menace of war?"

PSYCHOANALYTIC CONCEPTS

Dream

For Freud, the dream is an activity of mental life that occurs during sleep and displays similarities with the waking state. The dream is not a somatic phenomenon but a psychological one. A dream, or more properly the recounting of a dream, is the distorted and veiled communication of latent content. This latent content is provided by things that are repressed during the course of the day (or a longer period of time) and are displaced into the unconscious. The dream is a world of its own and a story of its own—the part of the world of mental life that can only unfold in a sleeping state.

Drive

Freud defines drives as the energies that derive from the needs of the id. Drives are the final cause of all activity. The drive is not an energy that reacts to the stimulation of the exterior world, but that comes from inside the organism.

The drive (*Trieb* in German) is not equatable with instinct. However, the use of the latter term in the most widely read English translation of Freud's writings has caused continuing confusion and debate. The drive consists of a biological drive source, a drive energy, and a drive aim that wants to be satisfied so that its energy can be discharged (pleasure). In his late work Freud posited two fundamental opposing drives: the libido (sex drive) and the death drive, i.e., Eros and Thanatos.

Parapraxis (Freudian Slip)

Freud proved that seemingly meaningless and senseless erroneous actions such as slips of the tongue, blunders, and oversights serve to fulfill unconscious wishes. The parapraxis, known in everyday language as the Freudian slip, is a compromise formation between an action's conscious intention and the simultaneous partial realization of an unconscious wish.

The Psychical Apparatus: Id, Ego, and Superego

The Ego and the Id was published in 1923. In it Freud sets out a conceptual organization of the "psychical apparatus." The psyche begins its development as an unorganized id (literally "it") from which the ego develops in its interaction with its surroundings (socialization). Lastly the superego develops out of the ego. The superego is to a certain degree a product of the parental relationship and its influence. Freud suggested the following visualization for his model: the horse (id), rider (ego), and riding master (superego).

Libido

The concept of libido does not represent conscious sexual desire but rather an economic principle including everything that "can be subsumed within love." Libido is energy and thus is a dynamic expression of the biological within the psyche.

Sexuality

In psychoanalysis the concept of sexuality is defined much more broadly than it is in general everyday language. Psychoanalysis operates under the premise that adult sexual behavior has a predecessor in childhood. This infantile sexuality develops in clearly definable phases and is of great importance in determining the sexuality of the adult.

"Psychoanalysis reckons as belonging to 'sexual life'," writes Freud "all the activities of the tender feelings which have primitive sexual impulses as their source, even when those impulses have become inhibited in regard to their original sexual aim or have exchanged this aim for another which is no longer sexual. For this reason we prefer to speak of *psychosexuality*, thus laying stress on the point that the mental factor in sexual life should not be overlooked or underestimated. We use the word 'sexuality' in the same comprehensive sense as that in which the German language uses the word *lieben* ['to love']."

Pleasure Principle/Reality Principle

Freud assumes that the purpose of all psychical activity is to prevent unpleasure (pain) and obtain pleasure. Unpleasure arises through the growth of drive tensions, whose discharge is experienced as pleasure.

In contrast, the reality principle states that the discharge of a drive must all too often be hindered or delayed, so that achievement of satisfaction (pleasure) is postponed or is never realized. Thus the reality principle serves as a regulator of the pleasure principle.

*The Committee, 1922. First row, from left: Sigmund Freud, Sandor Ferenczi, Hanns
Sachs. Standing, from left: Otto Rank, Karl Abraham, Max Eitingon, Ernest Jones*
Courtesy of Multiart.

6

Colleagues and Patients

Helmut Strutzmann

KEY FIGURES AROUND FREUD

Carl Gustav Jung (1875–1961) was a student of Sigmund Freud and is considered to be the founder of analytic (or complex) psychology. He is also often referred to as the "mystic among the fathers of psychoanalysis." The Swiss psychiatrist was, along with Sigmund Freud and Alfred Adler, one of the founders of depth psychology. He turned against Freud's concept of infantile sexuality as the source of the libido and emphasized the general will to love.

Alfred Adler (1870–1937) is considered to be the founder of individual psychology. From 1902 to 1911 he was a colleague and ally of Sigmund Freud, but thereafter he developed into a critic and opponent of Freudian psychoanalysis. He was one of the founding members of the Wednesday Psychological Society, from which he later resigned to found the Society for Individual Psychology.

Ernest Jones (1879–1958) became Freud's "official biographer." He is deemed to have been the founder of Freud's "Secret Committee." In 1910 he founded the American Psychopathological Association and a year later the American Psychoanalytic Association. His research focused on the psychoanalytic theory of symbols. Jones and Freud remained friends throughout their lives, and Jones delivered the eulogy at Freud's funeral.

Otto Rank (1881–1939) developed the theory of birth trauma, in which the child experiences its own birth as a shock that can have psychological consequences in cases where the individual is not able to deal with it.

Josef Breuer (1842–1925) developed a new talk therapy for treating hysteria, in which symptoms could be made to disappear when their cause or the incidents surrounding their first appearance were recalled to memory and their accompanying affects thus abreacted. Together with Sigmund Freud he authored the publications "On the Psychical Mechanism of Hysterical Phenomena" (1893) and *Studies on Hysteria* (1895), which represented the end of their working relationship.

Marie Bonaparte (1882–1962) was the great granddaughter of Lucien Bonaparte, the brother of Napoleon Bonaparte. In 1925 she consulted Freud in Vienna and began an analysis. After her return to Paris in 1926 she decided to devote herself completely to psychoanalysis and its dissemination. In 1938 she succeeded with the aid of American Ambassador W. C. Bullitt in obtaining an exit visa from occupied Austria for Sigmund Freud and enabling him to relocate in London. In addition to translating numerous Freud writings, she herself published a formidable oeuvre, including works on Edgar Allen Poe, drive theory, and female sexuality.

Anna Freud (1895–1982) was Sigmund Freud's youngest daughter. She underwent her training analysis with her father and went into practice as an analyst. Her work was concentrated primarily on children. She and Melanie Klein are considered to be the founders of child analysis.

Helene Deutsch, nee Rosenbach (1884–1982) was Freud's assistant, and he had a major influence on her. Her special areas of interest were the psychology of women and feminine sexuality. In addition to her scientific work, Helene Deutsch was also a political activist and a campaigner for women's rights.

Melanie Klein (1882–1960) was of Hungarian descent. Her training analysts and mentors were Sándor Ferenczi and Karl Abraham. In her theoretical work, Melanie Klein revolutionized the Freudian theory of the Oedipus complex by positing decisive processes, such as the development of guilt feelings and of the superego, much earlier in life than Freud did.

THE PSYCHOANALYTIC ASSOCIATION

At the beginning of the twentieth century, a group of colleagues and interested persons met weekly in Berggasse for the purpose of discussing Freud's theories and his practical experiences. These "Wednesday meetings" were the forerunner of the "Psychoanalytic Association," which exists to this day. Among the association's first members were numerous important researchers, including Alfred Adler, Wilhelm Stekel, Paul Federn, Eduard Hitschmann, and Ernest Jones. In April 1906, the first Congress for Freudian Psychology took place. It was organized by C. G. Jung, who would later break with Freud.

During the following years congresses of psychoanalysts were held regularly, and psychoanalytic societies were formed in many countries. Freud's contradictory nature can be seen in the fact that many of his followers turned away from him over the years because they did not adhere to his theories and instead went their own scientific and analytic ways.

PATIENTS AND CASE HISTORIES

Dora

The eighteen-year-old Dora suffered from a nervous cough, asthmatic symptoms, occasional loss of her voice and other complaints. Her parents' marriage was less than happy. Her father had a mistress, whose husband had attempted to seduce Dora. She had rejected his advances, but nevertheless Freud maintained that she had a repressed sexual desire for him and also for her own father and even for his mistress. Freud derived this constellation from two of his patient's dreams, which he interpreted with her.

The Rat Man

From October 1907 through January 1908, Freud treated a twenty-nine-year-old Viennese lawyer (Ernst Lanzer). The man had suffered since his childhood under obsessions that had steadily become worse. He feared that something terrible could happen to his father and to a woman he much admired. Freud discovered that the obsessions had begun after an officer had told his patient that in the Orient it was a common punishment to tie a pot of living rats onto a man's buttocks. The patient feared that his father—who was actually already dead—and the woman he admired could be subjected to this rat torture.

In this fear Freud saw the reversal of a death wish toward the father, who had often struck his son and who the patient felt had been a hindrance in his sexual development. After a few months of treatment, the imagination of the "rat punishment" had dissolved.

The Wolf Man

After years of unsuccessful treatment in a variety of European hospitals, the twenty-three-year-old Russian Sergei Pankejeff was considered a hopeless case. Freud gave his patient the memorable title "Wolf Man" because as a small boy he had dreamed that white wolves were sitting in the tree before his window and wanted to eat him. He suffered from this wolf phobia for six years. Freud derived this early disturbance from a seduction of the boy by his sister during childhood and from the fact that at the age of one and a half he had seen his parents engaged in sexual intercourse.

After four years of unsuccessful treatment, Freud informed his patient that he planned to conclude the analysis. This threat caused the Wolf Man to give up his resistances and led to a successful completion of the analysis.

Bruno Walter

The legendary orchestra conductor and composer Bruno Walter consulted Freud in 1906 because of a cramp in his right arm which he feared was the beginning of a paralysis that would interfere with his work. At Freud's advice, Walter spent some time in the South resting. But upon his return, his condition had only slightly improved. Nonetheless, Freud counseled him not to stop conducting. Walter took Freud's advice and resumed his work. He also underwent several analysis sessions.

7

Unveiling the Twenty-First Century

Helmut Strutzmann

SIGMUND FREUD AND THE DISILLUSIONMENT

Copernicus—Darwin—Freud

In the course of history, three great thinkers and discoverers have robbed human beings of their illusions of omnipotence, thus making key contributions to the further development of human society.

- Nicolaus Copernicus denied human beings the illusion that the earth stands at the center of the universe.
- Charles Darwin dispelled the illusion of human uniqueness by proving that the human race is a result of an evolutionary development.
- Sigmund Freud dispelled the illusion that human beings rule over their own thoughts and actions. According to Freud, human behavior is driven by the unconscious.

To this day, all three of these thinkers never cease to fascinate and to give rise to resistance and contradiction—even though their theories have long since been proven as reality

Freud's theory of the unconscious is more relevant today than ever, in an era when his theories on war and mass psychology appear in a new light and his fragmentation of the soul allows associations to the interactive world of digital technology.

This demonstrates the great significance of Sigmund Freud. He can continually be interpreted anew and put into new contexts.

Freud's Arrival in Paris, 1938, with Marie Bonaparte and the American Ambassador
William C. Bullit
Courtesy of Multiart.

SIGMUND FREUD: LIFE AND HISTORY

1856 Sigmund Freud is born in Pribor (today in the Czech Republic).

1859 Move to Vienna.

1865 Admission to the Gymnasium in Vienna's second district.

1873 Freud decides to study medicine. He reads *Oedipus Rex* for his final exams.

1877 First publications, including "Intersexuality Among Eels."

1881 Freud takes his doctorate in medicine.

1882 Engagement to Martha Bernays.

1882–1885 Work at the Vienna General Hospital.

1884–1887 Self-experiments with cocaine.

1885–1886 Studies under Charcot at the Salpetriere, Paris. Charcot opens new insights into hysteria and hypnosis.

1886 Freud goes into private practice and marries Martha Bernays.

1887 Work with hypnosis.

1891 Writings on aphasia, speech disorders and neurology.

1893–1996 Work with Josef Breuer (*Studies on Hysteria*).

1895 Birth of daughter Anna Freud.

1896 Death of Freud's father. The term "psychoanalysis" is used for the first time.

1897 Beginning of Freud's self-analysis.

1899 *The Interpretation of Dreams* is published (dated 1900).

1902 Founding of the "Wednesday Psychological Society."

1905 Publication of *Three Essays on the Theory of Sexuality, Jokes and Their Relation to the Unconscious*, and the "Dora" case study.

1906 Friendship with Carl Gustav Jung.

1908 First international congress of psychoanalysts in Salzburg.

1909 Freud and Jung travel to the United States and hold the first lectures on psychoanalysis.

1912 Jung returns to the United States.

1912–1913 *Totem and Taboo* is published; break with Jung.

1915–1917 Freud holds a series of introductory lectures on psychoanalysis.

1919 Freud analyzes men traumatized in war.

1920 Death of daughter Sophie. *Beyond the Pleasure Principle* is published First congress of psychoanalysts following the war.

1921 *Group Psychology and the Analysis of the Ego* is published.

1923 Freud is diagnosed with cancer. Death of Freud's favorite grandchild Heinerle.

1927 *The Future of an Illusion* is published.

1930 *Civilization and Its Discontents* is published.

1932 "Why War?"—published correspondence with Albert Einstein.
1933 Freud's books are burned.
1936 Eightieth birthday. Freud is honored by the Royal Society in Britain.
1938 Emigration to London.
1939 Freud dies in London on 23 September.
1942 Freud's sister Adolphine dies in the concentration camp Theresienstadt.
   Mitzi, Rosa, and Paula—Freud's other sisters—are deported to the concentration camp Treblinka and are murdered.

SIGMUND FREUD: LIFE AND HISTORY

1856 Treaty of Paris ends the Crimean War. Birth of George Bernard Shaw
   and Woodrow Wilson. Death of Heinrich Heine.
1859 Charles Darwin publishes *The Origin of Species*. Third edition of
   Schopenhauer's *The World as Will and Representation*. Construction of the
   Suez Canal begins. Austria is at war with Piedmont.
1861–1865 American Civil War.
1863 Founding of the International Red Cross in Geneva.
1865 Gregor Mendel discovers the laws of genetic inheritance.
1868 The first plastic (celluloid) is produced by John W. Hyatt. The dry cell
   is patented by George Leclanche.
1875–1876 The telephone is invented by Alexander Graham Bell.
1876 The internal combustion engine is designed by Nikolaus August Otto.
1877 Edison's gramophone.
1878 Mayerling Affair: the heir to the Austrian throne commits suicide.
1881 Robert Koch discovers the tuberculosis bacillus.
1885 Carl Benz and Gottlieb Daimler construct the first automobile.
1886 Unveiling of the Statue of Liberty in New York.
1889 Opening of the Eiffel Tower for the International Expo in Paris.
1894 The Dreyfus Affair: a wave of anti-Semitism breaks out in France.
1895 First public cinema presentation in Paris. Wilhelm Conrad Röntgen discovers x-rays. Kodak begins manufacturing cameras. Oscar Wilde is arrested because of his homosexuality.
1898 First "wireless" telegram is transmitted.
1900 Blood types are discovered by Karl Landsteiner. Arthur Schnitzler's *La
   Ronde* causes a scandal in Berlin. Death of Friedrich Nietzsche.
1902 Lenin writes "What Is to Be Done?"
1904 Russo-Japanese War. Ivan Petrovich Pavlov receives the Nobel Prize for
   his work on the physiology of digestion.
1905 Albert Einstein's theory of relativity. Alfred Binet's first intelligence
   test.

1908 Austria-Hungary annexes Bosnia-Herzegovina. Pablo Picasso and Georges Braque originate Cubism.

1913 First Charlie Chaplin film.

1914–1918 World War I.

1917 Russian Revolution.

1919 Treaty of Versailles.

1920 First meeting of the League of Nations. The National Socialist Party is founded in Germany. First admission of women to Oxford University.

1921 Founding of the BBC.

1923 Economic depression in Germany and Austria. The Ruhr is occupied by France and Belgium.

1925 Hitler's *Mein Kampf* is published in Germany.

1926 General strike in England.

1927 Charles Lindbergh flies solo over the Atlantic.

1929 Stock market crash on Wall Street. Alexander Fleming discovers penicillin.

1933 Hitler comes to power. Burning of the Reichstag and book burnings in Germany.

1934 Engelbert Dollfuss, the Austro-fascist chancellor, is murdered by the Nazis.

1935 Enactment of the Nuremberg Race Laws.

1936–1939 Spanish Civil War.

1938 Munich Accord. Annexation of Austria by Germany.

1939 Outbreak of World War II.

Freud, ca. 1938
Courtesy of Multiart.

8

Freud and Literature and Art

Helmut Strutzmann

Throughout his life, Sigmund Freud occupied himself with literature in the context of his psychoanalytic work: his study of Shakespeare's plays (*Lear* and *Hamlet*), his discussion of Jensen's novel *Gradiva,* and his exploration of Dostoevsky and patricide remain to this day not only impressive scholarly essays but also demonstrate the high literary quality of Freud's work. His correspondence with Albert Einstein, "Why War?" is also worthy of mention in this context.

Conversely, many literati have shown great interest in Freud and have been inspired by him in their work: Thomas Mann, Stefan and Arnold Zweig, indirectly Arthur Schnitzler, André Gide, the French Surrealists and the Existentialists, great masters of the psychological novel like Robert Musil, and also Virginia Woolf, the Scandinavian authors, and American novelists of the post–World War II era.

An excerpt from a speech given at Freud's eightieth birthday that was signed by hundreds of writers, artists, and friends:

> We, who could not possibly imagine the mental world in which we live without Freud's daring life's work, are happy to know that this great and tireless man is still among us and to see him continuing his work with undiminished energy. May our thankful feelings accompany the honoured man long into the future.

FREUD AND THE FINE ARTS

Sigmund Freud viewed Michelangelo's *Moses* statue in Rome about three thousand times. He loved his Egyptian miniatures, depictions of the Sphinx, and the buildings of the Renaissance, which he described in detail in various letters.

His studies on Leonardo (childhood memories) and Michelangelo are just as fascinating as psychoanalytic interpretations of contemporary artworks.

Several generations of artists have invoked the name of Sigmund Freud: the Surrealists and the Dadaists, great masters such as René Magritte, Marcel Duchamp, and Andy Warhol, Max Ernst, Giorgio de Chirico, the Symbolists, and Pop Artists of the postwar era, and most of all Salvador Dalí and Paul Klee.

In painting, the exploration of the unconscious, repressed sexuality, the psyche as a metaphor, and the dream represent a well-trodden path in the art history of the twentieth century. One of Sigmund Freud's grandchildren, Lucien Freud, is considered to be one of the most important figurative painters of the late twentieth century.

Freud himself enjoyed drawing and did so often. Indirectly, his sketches are also an expression of his unconscious.

Freud is often caricatured and—as if his work on the joke were being illustrated after the fact—used as the personification of psychoanalysis in the many satirical depictions of it, which form a genre of humor that has itself become a part of everyday life.

SIGMUND FREUD AND THE AVANT-GARDE

The Sigmund Freud Foundation in Vienna, which also operates the Freud Museum in Berggasse, has shown great dedication in inviting contemporary artists to deal with Freud and psychoanalysis in their work. Thus a number of internationally recognized works of art have been created and donated to the museum. They are permanently exhibited in the Sigmund Freud Museum in Vienna, forming an exciting contrast to the facility's other exhibits.

Among the participating artists are many well-known persons: Jenny Holzer, Joseph Kossuth, John Baldessari, Georg Herold, Pierpaolo Calzolari, Ilya Kabakov, and Franz West.

9

Freud and the Twenty-First Century

Helmut Strutzmann

In the early years of the twenty-first century, the reacceptance of Freud's concepts has been considerable. Numerous books have been and continue to be published on the occasion of the 150th anniversary of Freud's birth. Simultaneously, the language-theoretical debate surrounding Freud and the reinterpretation initiated by Jacques Lacan, Félix Guattari, and Gilles Deleuze (anti-Oedipus) have achieved a new level of quality. Freud's semiotic significance, as well as his literary and narrative power, are being discovered anew.

In view of the increase in religious conflict and religiously motivated war, Freud's analyses of religion—such as *Moses and Monotheism* and *Totem and Taboo*—have a new present-day relevance.

THE DREAM AND MODERN CREATIVITY RESEARCH

Sigmund Freud interpreted the dream as the fulfillment of a repressed wish from childhood. However, he was himself forced to admit that certain dreams do not fit in with this theory. Today, leading scientists also tend to see dreaming as a creative activity, as a part of the learning process, as a function of fantasy, as a form of information processing that occurs during sleep. Empirical findings in sleep laboratories and the discoveries of neuroscience modify and extend Sigmund Freud's dream concept into a more complex theory of the unconscious. Dreams are creative information processing in sleep. Physicians no longer shy away from speaking of repression in the context of meticulous descriptions of disease symptoms, nor from analyzing patients' dreams in psychoanalytic sessions.

Freud at Desk, 1938
Courtesy of Multiart.

However, at those points where computer tomography's ability to make a meaningful statement has been exhausted, some researchers return to the conventional methods of psychoanalysis. Infant research has proven the fundamental importance of early childhood—one of Freud's key principles. Today, brain researchers are able to explain the causes of "infantile amnesia," a term coined by Freud to describe the forgetting of the earliest childhood experiences. Neurobiologists have discovered the dopamine circuit, the so-called award system, which demonstrates great similarity to Freud's description of the libido.

Ironically, it seems that the neurosciences, which toppled Freud from his pedestal, will be paving the way for his renaissance in the twenty-first century.

THE LIBIDINOUS SOCIETY OF FEAR

There are still new sides of Sigmund Freud's thinking that remain to be discovered: for example the Freud who analyzed our contradictory wishes, our fixations and obsessions. And then there is the Freud who dealt not only with Eros but also with Thanatos.

"Sex was yesterday"—this is not only the realization that today we are drifting into a neobourgeois prudery, which is exemplified in many Western countries by the denial of access for teenagers to vaccinations against certain sexual diseases in order to force them to remain chaste. It is not only the diagnosis that sexual desire has become fragmented by Internet pornography and telephone sex—it is also the victory of Thanatos over Eros.

Today, the subliminal motto in many civilized countries is "Make war, not love." Seen from a global perspective, it seems that the sexual libido is undergoing a transformation into a lust for violence—a paradigm shift that Freud already discerned in the context of World War I and the rise of Nazism. Fear is increasingly being used to steer political decisions. It was the later Freud who reflected on the human animal's inclination toward aggression in *Civilization and Its Discontents*, a phenomenon that is urgently in need of our attention. "When sex again becomes a private matter, and death a public one, then there is a whole lot to be done on the global couch" (*Cicero*, 2006). "Sex war gestern" (Sex Was Yesterday)

If civilization imposes such great sacrifices not only on man's sexuality, but on his aggressivity, we can understand better why it is hard for him to be happy in that civilization. In fact, primitive man was better off in knowing no restrictions of instinct. To counterbalance this, his prospects of enjoying this happiness for any length of time were very slender. Civilized man has exchanged a portion of his possibilities of happiness for a portion of security. (Sigmund Freud, *Civilization and Its Discontents*)

CIVILIZATION AND ITS DISCONTENTS

The fateful question for the human species seems to me to be whether and to what extent their cultural development will succeed in mastering the disturbance of their communal life by the human instinct of aggression and self-destruction. It may be that in this respect precisely the present time deserves a special interest. Men have gained control over the forces of nature to such an extent that with their help they would have no difficulty in exterminating one another to the last man. They know this, and hence comes a large part of their current unrest, their unhappiness and their mood of anxiety. And now it is to be expected that the other of the two 'Heavenly Powers', eternal Eros, will make an effort to assert himself in the struggle with his equally immortal adversary. But who can foresee with what success and with what result?

In these sentences Freud anticipated the coming to power of fascism and National Socialism. His theories are just as valid with regard to the conflicts of the twenty-first century. They hold true for the disputes in the Middle East just as much as they do for the conflicts in Latin America and Africa that are arising due to economic exploitation. In the end, many of the catastrophes of nature are nothing more than a result of the "human desire to master the powers of nature," a retaliation for economically oriented interventions.

HATE IN THE TWENTY-FIRST CENTURY

Freud's thesis that the "civilized human being" represents the sublimation of aggression and of the death drive, which the instinctual human being can live out without limitation, is of relevance today and is a subject of debate as it was during Freud's lifetime.

The fact is, as is shown by present-day studies and investigations, that aggression is rising worldwide and that there are links between the breaking of cultural taboos and restraints and an explosion of aggression.

In his book *Le discours de la haine* (The Discourse of Hate), published in 2004, the French philosopher and social critic André Glucksmann makes frequent references to Freud and his theory of Eros and Thanatos. Glucksmann argues that hate—Freud would call it the aggressive instinct—occupies a dominant position as an irrational phenomenon in most social disputes of the current era.

The declarations of war leading to the First World War, the unexpected enthusiasm, the general euphoria of the mobilization turned material, economic and social structures upside down. Civilians were struck a blow in body and soul, in their convictions and beliefs. The unimaginable downfall of all values only became apparent gradually and at a later time. Freud was one of the first, in 1915, to discern the astonishing 'disappointments,' the rejection of all 'limitations . . . which are observed and honoured in times of peace.' The 'blind rage' that is hidden within our civilization 'throws down that which stands in its (war's) way . . . as if there would be no future and no peace for humanity after its end.' And the inventor of psychoanalysis discovered a mysterious 'death drive' at the heart of human nature. It functions silently, beyond the pleasure principle, hidden under the allure and guile of Eros." (Glucksman, 2004)

THE CURRENT RELEVANCE OF EROS AND THANATOS

Hardly any other Freud writing met with the resistance elicited by *Beyond the Pleasure Principle*. Freud's late realization that it is not the sex drive alone that dominates human behavior but also its antagonist, the death drive, that exerts just as much of an influence, disturbed even his closest adherents.

For Freud, Thanatos is a mute drive. According to Freud, the preservation of life and civilization is only possible within a mixture of the life (libido) and death drive. Overcoming the death drive is the mission of every civilized society, Freud stated, and religion is not in a position to achieve such ends.

Freud's realization, which also represented a radical break with the biologism of his era although it actually derived from them, was confirmed by the conflicts dominating the world at the time.

The irrational aspects of conflicts with and aggression against the Other— the Other had a key position in Freud's thinking—are readily apparent today, as is the reinstatement of religion as an explanation for aggressive conflicts. As Glucksmann wrote:

Hate comes clothed as love. Does not hate invoke commiseration and the preservation of harmony and light-heartedness as a pretext for excluding and killing? . . . Hate disguises itself in alibis. Maybe I am mistaken, he might admit, but I meant well. I have good intentions and am not at all evil. He who accuses me of evilness is the one that is unsound. (Glucksmann, 2004)

FREUD IN EVERYDAY LIFE

Hardly ever has the work of any other scientist, in its concepts and linguistic inventions, become so clearly anchored in everyday language as that of Sigmund Freud.

A multitude of theoretical impulses mark the "submerged cultural legacy" of completely accepted figures of speech and thought. We use concepts like subconscious, unconscious, superego, repression, and trauma without a second thought. And even though the use of such words may be unreflected, our self-understanding has long since accepted the notion that the human psyche is complex and vulnerable and that collective psychical processes must also be observed carefully.

A look into the search engine Google produces numbers that seem nearly inconceivable and quantitatively put Freud on the level of a pop star or a top athlete. The term psychoanalysis comes up 12.1 million times, while Sigmund Freud produces a list of 9.45 million entries. *The Interpretation of Dreams* comes up with 12.6 million entries, and "libido" generates 13.3 million results.

Of course Freudian terminology has been watered down in everyday language. It is hardly subject to any deliberation and also does not necessarily reflect the dimensions that Freud was thinking in when he created it.

Freud is—and this can be seen in the numerous essays and commentaries that are being published on the 150th anniversary of his birth—still a personality that elicits contradiction, a "thorn in the flesh," to cite the French Nobel Prize winner Jean-Paul Sartre.

THE PSYCHE AND DIGITAL TECHNOLOGY

There are astonishing parallels between psychoanalytic work and the digitization of information.

In psychoanalytic work, the analyst destroys the patient's self. That which seems to be a closed system within itself is broken down into elementary parts and fragments and is put together again.

Digitization is not any different; it is also a fragmentation of information followed by a reassembly. The French psychoanalyst Jacques Lacan in the 1950s already viewed the unconscious as a structure that functions like a language. This structure is comparable to digital data and knowledge archives that are seemingly virtual and "in the dark" until they again become visible through the application of technology. Thus the anarchic, unstructured Internet resembles the unconscious, just as dreams are also a textual processing of the day's events in their own grammar.

Lacan's later writings provide an answer to the problems involved in establishing the "true self". Harking back to Freud, who saw the id as the actual "core of our being," Lacan postulates: There, where the id speaks, is the location of the "true" subject as a subject of the unconscious and not of self-consciousness, as a subject of the symbolic and not of the imaginary.

MANIFESTO

"Where id was, there shall ego be." The language of the unconscious remains to be deciphered. The concession that the ego and the conscious mind are not the masters of their own house but rather are continually under siege by our drives, the outer world and the superego with its norms and demands, and that the development of culture comes about through the renunciation of drives should in the twenty-first century no longer represent an affront to the self-certain ego-subject nor cause a society to live in fear of a loss of identity.

Sigmund Freud challenges us to have no fear of reason but rather of the repression of fear: we will never learn anything from the aggressiveness of the last Balkan War, the terrorism of our era, the conflict of values between the West and Islam, or the inhumanity of poverty in the Third World if we repress that which makes us afraid of them. We are not plain and simply rational: we are able to become so.

"The voice of the intellect is soft, but it does not rest until it has been heard." And yet reason also gives rise to the Other of itself as well. We are not well prepared to listen to it. Eros and Thanatos, the pleasure principle and the reality principle, stand in constant conflict. The id, ego, and superego are struggling for position, while drive renunciation and defense mechanisms are continually giving rise to new conflicts that can make us ill, as individuals and as a society.

Freud freed us from illusions, but he also evoked others and made them visible. He showed us the paths to self-insight—nearby in the mirror of another reflected. They should lead us to freedom and authenticity, just as he freed psychology from its commingling with physiological facts and opened the broad field of psychosomatics.

With Freud we have abandoned old thought patterns and strode forth out of modernism—we have learned to read autonomy, consciousness, the ego and rationality in a different way, as illusions and dreams as well. Freud taught us to be skeptical of ideologies, utopias and doctrines of salvation, a skepticism that the globalized world and the knowledge society of the twenty-first century urgently needs. We have to take the principle of skepticism seriously, because this principle alone justifies optimism.

Society, politics, and the economy are called upon to realize Freud's message in the twenty-first century, to respect the creativity and originality of every individual in a world becoming more anonymous, to stand up for Freud's contribution to the value of the individual in the face of industrial destruction, the attacks on the welfare state, the disintegration of systems of meaning, and the crisis of democracy.

The political system must confront Freud's insight that nationalism and xenophobia derive from primal urges, unconscious fantasies, and internal repressions, and also from the insight that limits must be set on desire and the economy's striving to increase profits.

The twenty-first century must assume that the repression and displacement of conflicts only gives rise to new conflicts. Precisely that which should not be must be recognized and not repressed. The manifesto is a challenge to take Freud's insights seriously.

Peter Kampits, professor of philosophy at the University of Vienna
Translation by Christopher Barber

FREUD'S PLACE IN OUR MINDS

*A Day of Reflection on Sigmund Freud's
Significance in the Twenty-First Century*

Freud at Desk, aquatint by May Pollak
Courtesy of Multiart.

10

Freud's Legacy

Never-Ending Questions

Judy Ann Kaplan

$\mathbf{F}$reud's legacy is his innovative method of investigation—his questioning—which led to a whole new way of seeing, hearing, understanding, and constructing meaning. Our challenge is to embrace this legacy by continuing to actively question our assumptions and observations, and allow ourselves the freedom to continue to see, hear, understand, and construct meaning in ever-evolving new ways.

With Freud, the unconscious, neurosis, narcissism, repression, regression, transference, and the repetition compulsion were discovered and conceptualized. Through Freud's questioning we learned the importance of listening—that the primacy of the patient's own words allows us to understand the patient's world, and that analytic listening is not only manifest content but cadence, rhythm, timing, sequence, parapraxes, and grammatical usage, as well as body movements. Through Freud's questioning we learned the importance of the association of events and the sequence of manifest content and how they reveal important information about unconscious and preconscious meanings. It is Freud's questioning which led him to make the connection between dreams and slips of the tongue.

Freud, always open to change, went on to develop new theories. In 1926 Freud offered this caveat: "It must not be supposed that these very general ideas are pre-suppositions on which the work of psychoanalysis depends. On the contrary, they are its latest conclusions and are open to revision. Psychoanalysis is founded securely upon the observation of the facts of mental life; and for that very reason its theoretical superstructure is . . . subject to constant alteration" (Freud, 1926).

Freud at first saw transference as a disruption in the treatment and felt that it interfered with free association and the recovery of memories. It was not

Freud, ca. 1907
Courtesy of Multiart.

until his treatment of Dora that he became aware of transference as an "inevitable necessity" for therapeutic action. Freud continued to add to the concept, and by 1920 transference had become the most important vehicle for exploring the vicissitudes of human passion. (J. Tucker, 1998)

When discussing the evolution of Freudian theory, Martin Bergmann talks about extenders, modifiers, and heretics. Heretics reach beyond their training analysis and continue self-analysis and make discoveries, and some even start their own schools, as Jung and Kohut did. Extenders develop Freudian theory, such as Nunberg and Waelder, and Modifiers change something substantial in theory while retaining the lineage, such as Hartmann. As a result, today the heritage of psychoanalysis is enormous; the number of schools multitudinous.

Our new challenge is to creatively explore the ongoing controversies. All kinds of questions emerge: What is analytic space? What is the nature of the transference? What is the real relationship? Are we a projection of the patient, or is the patient our projection? Is there any reality outside of the situation we are creating? How much is repetition from the past, which will lead to reconstructive work, and how much is a new relationship that is being formed in the present—the here and now? Do interpretations cure or does the relationship cure, or is it a combination of both? (C. Ellman, 1998)

As Freud said, asking the questions is far more important than the answers. Our work and Freud's legacy depend upon our curiosity and openness to the process, to the unknown, to whatever each individual analysand brings into the space we provide. It is the analytic frame, developed by Freud, that allows, through questioning, the deepening into a place where understanding joins creativity and conjures new shapes and patterns. In the spirit of Freud we must take risks, undergo conflict and change, and actively select in and select out in order to fully experience the joys and the creativity of the treatment process. Freud's legacy is the analytic space, and how we should remain creative within the analytic space.

To paraphrase Captain Kirk of *Star Trek*: Analytic Space . . . the ever-evolving frontier. These are the journeys of Freud's heirs. Our mission: To explore strange new worlds of the mind. To seek out new symbols and new meanings. To boldly question what no one has questioned before.

NOTES

Bergmann, M. S. (1993). Reflections on the history of psychoanalysis. *JAPA* 4:1, 929–55.

Ellman, C. (1998). Introduction. In *The Modern Freudians*, eds. C. Ellman, et al., pp. xxii–xxiii. Northvale, NJ: Jason Aronson.

Freud, S. (1905). Fragment of an analysis of a case of hysteria. *SE* 7:7–122.

———. (1912). The dynamics of transference. *SE* 12:97–120.

———. (1914). Remembering, repeating, and working through (further recommendations on the technique of psycho-analysis II). *SE* 12:145–56.

———. (1926). Psychoanalysis by Sigmund Freud. *The Encyclopedia Britannica*, 13th ed. Cambridge, UK: The University Press.

Tucker, J. (1998). Overview of controversies. In *The Modern Freudians*, eds. C. Ellman et al., pp. 123–24. Northvale, NJ: Jason Aronson.

Psychoanalysis and Psychosis

Ann-Louise S. Silver

While Freud said that personally he did not like working with people struggling with psychosis, many who did work with them found Freud's concepts extremely helpful. Ernst Simmel launched the first psychoanalytically oriented hospital at Tegelsee. I. H. Schultz at Weisser Hirsch introduced his young assistant, Frieda Fromm-Reichmann, to Freud's writings. As soon as she discovered his works on transference she knew this was central. She had sensed that there was something strange and important in the way patients idealized their doctors, and Freud made clear what was happening (Silver, p. 478; Hornstein, pp. 29–32).

Meanwhile, doctors at hospitals in the United States were discovering Freud (Silver, 2002). Adolf Meyer, who had trained at the Burghölzli Clinic in Zurich, was the preeminent psychiatrist in the United States at the time that Freud, Jung, and Ferenczi came to the Clark University 20th Anniversary Conference in 1909. Freud was amazed to discover how much his ideas had already influenced those in attendance and those presenting. The conference attendees had come to meet the man whose writings had so influenced their work. William Alanson White and Smith Ely Jelliffe and their wives made trips to Europe each summer starting the following year. They met with the European pioneers in psychoanalysis and brought back their papers which they translated during the return trip. They summarized the German journals, all of this published in America's first psychoanalytic journal, *Psychoanalytic Review*, which began in 1913. Unfortunately, its first issue included C. G. Jung's long paper in which he officially split from Freud, "The Theory of Psychoanalysis."

White was the superintendent of the federal mental hospital, St. Elizabeths, in Washington, D.C. His staff contributed significantly to his journal, which thus has a heavy and fascinating emphasis on psychosis and psychoanalytic approaches. Harry Stack Sullivan joined the staff of St. Elizabeths in 1921.

I want to relate Sullivan's one-genus postulate, which one can trace directly to White and from White to people who heard Freud speak at Clark University.

> I now want to present what I used to call the one-genus hypothesis, or postulate. This hypothesis I word as follows: We shall assume that everyone is much more simply human than otherwise, and that anomalous interpersonal situations, insofar as they do not arise from differences in language or custom, are a function of differences in relative maturity of the persons concerned . . . I have become occupied with the science, not of individual differences, but of human identities, or parallels . . . I try to study the degrees and patterns of things which I assume to be ubiquitously human. [So much for mouse models of schizophrenia!] (Sullivan, 1953)

We need to remember this now, in our current biological medicalized era in which people with schizophrenia are thought to suffer from some incurable and relentless brain disease requiring medications. These agents block dopamine pathways, impeding limbic system connections with the cortex. They thus have a powerful dampening effect on salience, defined by Kapur as "a process whereby events and thoughts come to grab attention, drive action, and influence goal-directed behavior . . ." (Kapur, 2003, p. 14). This loss of verve, sense of wonder at a natural scene, or pleasure in a new insight or interpersonal connection is intolerable for at least 75 percent of patients, who discontinue their medications within two years (Psychiatry24x7.com, sponsored by Janssen Pharmaceuticals).

Frieda Fromm-Reichmann arrived in the United States in 1935, working at the now closed Chestnut Lodge in Rockville. She formed an immediate affinity for Sullivan, and they worked closely together. Her book, *Principles of Intensive Psychotherapy* is a classic, in continuous print since 1950. She stressed methods by which therapists could enhance and develop their empathic potential, building upon their respect for the patient. She echoed Sullivan in saying, "Such respect can be valid only if the psychiatrist realizes that his patient's difficulties in living are not too different from his own." (Fromm-Reichmann, 1950, p. xi) "Where there is lack of security, there is anxiety; where there is anxiety, there is fear of the anxieties in others. The insecure psychiatrist is, therefore, liable to be afraid of his patients' anxiety." (Fromm-Reichmann, 1950, p. 24) In a Lodge seminar on intuition, she said to a therapist:

> To your problem of feel(ing) guilty if one doesn't understand, I had recently an idea about that—that the not being able to understand, that is, somebody communicating with us and we not understanding, in general connotes loneliness. If

we don't understand, that touches on our own possibilities of loneliness, and rather than accepting there is this barrier of loneliness between the psychotic and us, we evade that and feel guilty. I think that the guilt feeling is an evasion of accepting the tragic facts of human loneliness." (Unpublished seminar on intuition in treating schizophrenia, p. 998)

Today, almost all of the psychodynamic hospitals in the United States have been forced to close, and the few remaining rely heavily on medication regimens as well as psychotherapy. Therapists around the country are suffering their own loneliness, isolation, and now, with the murder of Wayne Fenton, by a patient for whom he was consulting on Sunday, September 3, 2006, anxiety as well. We have formed a nonprofit organization, growing out of the triennial International Symposia on the Psychotherapy of Schizophrenia, launched in 1956 by Gaetanno Benedetti and Christian Müller, both of whom trained at the Burghölzli. ISPS-US welcomes everyone who is interested in this topic, whether they actually treat patients suffering from psychosis or not. Please visit our website (www.isps-us.org). We value our members who have recovered from psychosis, among whom is our board member, Joanne Greenberg, author of *I Never Promised You a Rose Garden*, and our active member, Catherine Penney (Dorman).

NOTES

Benedetti, G. (1995). *Psychotherapy of Schizophrenia*. Northvale, NJ: Jason Aronson, reissue.

Dorman, D. (2003). *Dante's Cure: A Journey Out of Madness*. New York: Other Press.

Fenton, Wayne. For information on this murder case, see "In the Line of Duty: A Special Report," part of the PBS series *The Infinite Mind*, broadcast beginning September 6, 2006, www.lcmedia.com/mind443.htm; Treatment Advocacy Center, psychlaws.blogspot.com/search/label/Wayne%20Fenton, a site that gives links to many other relevant articles; Psychiatry On Line, pn.psychiatryonline.org/cgi/content/full/41/19/1

Fromm-Reichmann, F. (1950). *Principles of Intensive Psychotherapy*. Chicago: University of Chicago Press.

Greenberg, J. (or Hannah Green) (1964). *I Never Promised You a Rose Garden*. New York: Holt, Rinehart & Winston.

Hornstein, G. (2000). *To Redeem One Person is to Redeem the World: The Life of Frieda Fromm-Reichmann*. New York: The Free Press.

Jung, C. G. (1914). "The theory of psychoanalysis," in W. A. White and S. E. Jelliffe, eds., *The Psychoanalytic Review: A Journal Devoted to an Understanding of Human Conduct*. New York: Journal of Nervous and Mental Disease Publishing Co., pp. 1–40, 153–77, 260–84, 415–30.

Kapur, S. (2003). "Psychosis as a state of aberrant salience: A framework linking biology, phenomenology, and pharmacology in schizophrenia." *American Journal of Psychiatry* 160: 13–23.

Silver, A-L., ed. P. C. (1989). *Psychoanalysis and Psychosis*. Madison, CT: International Universities Press.

———. (2002) "Psychoanalysis and psychosis: Players and history in the United States." *Psychoanalysis and History* 4(1), 45-66.

Sullivan, H. S. (1953). *The Interpersonal Theory of Psychiatry*. New York: W. W. Norton & Co.

Implications of Integrating
Psychoanalysis with Neuroscience

H. Michael Meagher

We all recall that Freud began his professional life as a neurologist. He did neuroanatomical research, wrote three monographs on the infantile cerebral paralyses of children, and wrote a monograph "On Aphasia." When he started a practice, he saw, as neurologists did then, both neurological and psychiatric patients. As he turned his attention to hysterical patients he tried to work out a neurological theory of hysteria, one grounded in the neurobiology of his day. This proved to be impossible given the state of biological knowledge at that time, so he assumed a purely psychological approach to theory and practice and created psychoanalysis. However he continued to believe that neuroses could be explained in biological terms:

> We must recollect that all of our provisional ideas in psychology will presumably one day be based on an organic substructure. (Freud, "On Narcissism," 1914)

> The deficiencies in our description would probably vanish if we were already in a position to replace the psychological terms with physiological or chemical ones. . . . We may expect (physics and chemistry) to give the most surprising information and we cannot guess what answers it will return in a few dozen years of questions we have put to it. They may be of a kind that will blow away the whole of our artificial structure of hypothesis. (Freud, "Beyond the Pleasure Principle" 1920)

Neuroscience—cognitive neuroscience, developmental neuroscience, affective neuroscience, and social neuroscience—has made great strides in "The Decade of the Brain," and it seems that the time is here for psychoanalysts to join with neuroscientists in exploring the mind-brain. The International

Neuro-Psychoanalysis Society has been founded. Eric Kandel has challenged us to bring our expertise in understanding the mind to the table both for examination and to enrich the biologist's appreciation for the workings of the mind. Many institutes are including neuroscience in their coursework, and more analysts are undertaking research. But many also have reservations. Some think that the neuroscientific findings will—or may—change our theory, but that it will have no effect on the practice of psychoanalysis. With this, there is a question about expending the effort to master a field that is not needed. However, it seems that neuroscience may already be influencing practice.

Mirror neurons are neurons that mirror similar neurons in another person (or primate) and which fire when the other person does something that we observe. If a monkey sees another monkey pick up a piece of food, the same neurons fire in the observing monkey as in the eating monkey. This seems to be a basis for empathy, imitation, and identification, and also is involved in language acquisition. In face-to-face therapy, analyst and analysand may be drawn into mirroring each other. Is free association possible in this circumstance? This may influence decisions about using the couch.

Neuroscience discredits infantile amnesia. Initially the infant and toddler only has procedural or implicit memory which is unconscious. Declarative memory takes longer to develop. Relationship patterns and moral learning are handled by procedural memory. Memory itself is always constructed. There may be more emphasis on understanding relationship patterns and associated fantasies and less on the recovery of repressed explicit memories.

Analysands vary in their cognitive capacities such as language abilities, long- and short-term memory, executive functioning, attention, and integration. Neuroscience has delineated more of the neural underpinnings of these skills. The analyst must know which are biologically based and which are the result of intrapsychic conflict in order to appropriately address the analysand's problems.

More is known about the various affect systems that come into play in analysis. Often psychoactive medication is used—appropriately—to address depression or anxiety.

This may facilitate the analysis by making the analysand more capable of working in analysis, less demoralized and fearful of becoming more symptomatic if he or she gets into certain areas.

Trauma has its own special biology that the analyst should understand and respect. It is important to recognize that the release of glucocorticoids during trauma may prevent the hippocampus from encoding the memory of the events leading to no memory, not a repressed one.

Complexity, not linear dynamics, underlies biological systems. Because of this, outcome cannot be absolutely predicted. This allows us to understand discontinuities in child development and it requires a loosening of the epigenetic model of development. It does not mean that all bets are off however. The neurosciences are here to stay, as is psychoanalysis. If we can work together we both will benefit.

NOTES

Freud, S. (1914). *On Narcissism: An Introduction*, SE 14:67–102.

———. (1920). *Beyond the Pleasure Principle*, SE 18:1–64.

Guttmann, G., and I. Scholz-Strasser, eds. (1998). *Freud and the Neurosciences: From Brain Research to the Unconscious*. Vienna: Verlag der Oesterreichischen Akademie dre Wissenschaften.

Kandel, E. R. (1999). Biology and the future of psychoanalysis: a new intellectual framework for psychiatry revisited. *American Journal of Psychiatry* 156: 505–534.

Olds, D. (2006). Interdisciplinary studies and our practice. *Journal of American Psychoanalytic Association* 54: 857–876.

Freud Is Everywhere

Marilyn S. Jacobs

Earlier this year, an Op Ed column in the *Los Angeles Times* asked the reader to "Imagine a day without Freud. . . . [because] . . . Freud is everywhere. . . ."[1]

This is an apt conclusion and is obviously not restricted to the vibrant community of psychoanalysis in Los Angeles.

A recent Google search of "Sigmund Freud" returned more than 800,000 results. "Sigmund Freud: 150th Anniversary" returned more than 3,800 results. Amazon.com lists over 31,000 books on the subject of "Freud."

Reflection upon the legacy of Sigmund Freud reveals a dichotomy. The legacy has been described by Harold Bloom as "the central imagination of our age" and by W. H. Auden as "a whole climate of opinion." Freud's theories about human nature have been the cornerstone of clinical mental health practice for over 100 years. Yet, there has also been a powerful debunking of Freud's ideas. As Peter Gay has noted, "There are no neutrals in the Freud wars." Criticism has proliferated. This ranges from Wittgenstein's view of psychoanalysis as "fanciful pseudo-explanation" to Janet Malcolm's conclusion of the paradoxical "uselessness of its insights."

As mental health professionals, the clinical problems we encounter in the twenty-first century are increasingly more complex, complicated, and intractable. We often feel powerless at the profound suffering we encounter. Although we benefit from breathtaking advances in science and technology, these advances often obfuscate our abilities and create new difficulties. We also face increasingly incomprehensible obstacles to human welfare. We struggle with the effects of globalization and economic instability, war, terrorism, ethnic strife, genocide, human rights abuses, social dislocations, environmental damage, and unprecedented cultural shifts.

The biobehavioral and social sciences, the realms from which these problems can be solved, favor empiricist methodology, conscious control, symptom reduction and behavioral change. These approaches are not always helpful to the issues at hand. Understanding the unconscious, phenomenology, context, meaning structures intersubjectivity, nonlinear systems, and relationality—approaches that could help—are largely sidelined.

Thus, the challenge of clinical treatment in the twenty-first century is to reintegrate psychoanalysis to the larger society. The four organizations represented here today have begun this task with considerable success. But there is a long way to go.

There is a great deal of optimism and a basis upon which to build. Psychoanalysis has undergone beneficial shifts since Freud and the first generations of psychoanalysts. A pluralism of rich ideas now informs psychoanalytic theory and practice. New roles have emerged. Many social institutions have taken notice. There is a revitalized creativity in understanding mental life.

I can speak personally to this undertaking. For the past fifteen years, I have worked to integrate psychoanalytic thinking into a highly technological medical subspecialty at an academic medical center. While I was initially met with skepticism, wariness, and unfamiliarity; (based largely on the absence of psychoanalysis from medical school curricula), my efforts have been successful at gaining trust, interest, and respect. My most compelling argument is the outcome: in the end, psychoanalysis is effective with medical patients.

We can foster renewal in the application of psychoanalysis to clinical work by redoubling our efforts at building bridges with the major social institutions. These would include of course medicine, but also education, child care, and the legal system. We will want to stress how we do not want to replace other traditions (such as cognitive behavioral therapy) but add to them.

Our task is to build on the genius of Freud's work while appreciating its limitations. We will also have to move beyond the Freud wars. We have the potential to make a change in our society and our world. We would be helped in this by thinking in terms of Karl Weik's theory of "small wins"[2] insofar as psychoanalysis is concerned and avoiding the hubris of ambition and overarching finalities.

Freud may be everywhere, but in clinical practice, he is not there quite nearly enough.

NOTES

1. Daum, M. (May 6, 2006) "Man of Our Dreams," *Los Angeles Times.*
2. Weick, K. (1984). Small wins: Redefining the scale of social problems. *American Psychologist* 39(1): 40-49.

New Challenges in Clinical Treatment

A Clinical Social Work Perspective

Golnar A. Simpson

In these early years of the twenty first century, we are at a point in our understanding of human functioning that instead of either/or dichotomies, we can begin having a more coherent conversation about the "seamlessness" of mind/body/context dynamics in health and in illness. From a clinical social work perspective, with our "person-in-environment" core orientation, and our historical and ongoing intimate relationship with psychoanalytic thought, Freud's contributions to this exciting process of discovery, analysis and synthesis is so enormous that it is hard to imagine getting to this point without him. It is in this holistic context and taking the "inclusiveness" (Shapiro, 2004, p. 332) of Freud's theory regarding psychology, biology, and social factors into account that I situate my brief comments on Freud's legacy and new challenges in treatment.

Now, a few words about the relationship between theory and practice. It is usually assumed that in clinical practice, theory and technique are informed by one another in a continuous circular fashion. Accordingly, treatment can be conceptualized as a process in which appropriate knowledge and skills provide the practitioner with a reasonable chance to gain access to the patient's meaning systems (conscious and unconscious) or internal world. Then, in the context of an empathic and trusting professional relationship, and with the help of appropriate techniques, we can move forward with the co-construction of new meanings and thus change and growth.

Freud, as a pioneer and scientist, utilized a variety of approaches to the discovery and unfolding of his theoretical formulations and his recommended techniques. Fonagy (2003) states that, as a neurologist, Freud was aware of the nonconscious workings of the brain and the importance of this fact in the development of psychopathology. This led Freud to put "two radical propositions" forward:

> First, mental health problems . . . may be understood in terms of certain non-consciously experienced mental states—that is beliefs and desires (Freud and Breuer, 1895). Second, the effective treatment of mental health problems could be undertaken if (and only if) the individual suffering from mental disorder was made aware of these nonconscious, and by definition maladaptive, beliefs and desires in an interpersonal context of considerable emotional intensity. (Freud, 1909, 1916, p. 30)

This of course is the elegant formulation about the therapeutic process that by now is accepted as a matter beyond argument. Regarding techniques, Freud freely acknowledged the fact that his recommended techniques were based on his years of personal experience and based on the fact that unwanted results had made him abandon other methods (Fonagy, 2003).

In psychoanalytic treatment, for a variety of reasons, the correspondence between theory and technique has not always been smooth. Today, with the diversity of theoretical schools, changing patient populations, and socioeconomic realities of practice, the situation has become even more complex and challenging. In this context, the metaphor of "developmental lag" proposed by Gray (2005, p. 30) to denote the relationship between ego theory and technique can also be used for other areas of the psychoanalytic theory and technique as well. However, it is also essential to remain aware of the positive aspects of this metaphor and the potential for enhancement of the creative tension necessary for narrowing the developmental lag and the integration of theory and technique. In my brief time with you, let me share some thoughts and propose a few questions regarding three important areas of Freud's legacy upon which we can build through our continuing examination and conversation.

THE UNCONSCIOUS

The first example has to do with the concept of the unconscious, where everything begins. Today, in addition to Freud's dynamic unconscious, there is also the neuroscience nonconscious with its processes not having the potential for becoming conscious; and/or a variety of other definitions such as the three realms of the unconscious comprised of the prereflective unconscious, the dynamic unconscious, and the unvalidated unconscious based on experience near intersubjective dynamics proposed by Stolorow and Atwood (1992). What are the implications of these different definitions for treatment process?

Are they compatible in any shape or form? In what ways do these different conceptualizations impact our way of listening for the unconscious material?

TRANSFERENCE

A second core related issue is the concept of transference. Today, cognitive neuroscience information (Westen and Gabbard, 2002) and elaborations of our clinical theories suggest that in addition to a global understanding of transference, it is more accurate and useful to consider a multiplicity of transferences related to the changing self-state dynamics of the participants in the moment to moment transactions involved in the treatment process. This requires appreciation for the complexity of the simultaneous mind/body/context dynamic transactions and the subjectivity and intersubjectivity of the participants. In this context, issues such as race, ethnicity, gender, life style, and other sociocultural factors present further challenges to the conceptualization of the dynamics of transference. Also, how about the role of language and the elaboration of Freud's ideas by Loewald (as cited in Mitchel, 2000) emphasizing the importance of the affective link that binds "language *in* primary process and language *in* secondary process"? (Mitchell, 2000, p. 8). How do we listen to the manifestations of the "conflictuality" which denote "the way in which the discourse alternately moves towards and away from a meaningful nucleus or a set of meaningful nuclei which are trying to enter consciousness" (Green, 2005, p. 43)? How do we discern the meaning of the messages that patients send to themselves (Green, 2005)? What are the implications of all of these processes for the different elements of technique? With all that is going on in the clinical encounter, how do we get to the "moment of meeting" defined as the therapist's "response beautifully adjusted to the situation immediately at hand"? (Stern, 2004, p. 169)

SOCIAL JUSTICE ISSUES

As a third and final comment, I would like to call attention to an aspect of Freud's legacy that is not often talked about: Freud's social activism and concerns with social justice issues. In a recent book titled: *Freud's Free clinics: Psychoanalysis and Social Justice, 1918–1938*, Elizabeth Danto, a social worker, tells the story of Freud and other first-generation analysts' establishment of free clinics such as the ambulatorium in Vienna and other European cities and developing a voucher system in lieu of money for the pro bono patients in order to protect their sense of pride and dignity. Danto, recounting

Freud's September 1918 speech before the fifth International Psychoanalytic Congress, states that:

> He invoked a set of modernist beliefs in achievable progress, secular society and the social responsibility of psychoanalysis. And he argued for the central role of government, the need to reduce inequality through universal access to services, the influence of the environment on individual behavior, and dissatisfaction with the status quo. (p. 17)

She follows with a direct quotation by Freud:

> It is possible to foresee that the conscience of the society will awake and remind it that the poor man should have just as much right to assistance for his mind as he now has to the life-saving help offered by surgery; and that neuroses threatens public health no less than tuberculosis and can be left as little as the latter to the impotent care of individual members of the community. (Jones, 1955, as cited in Danto, 2005, p. 17)

Today, universal, accessible, acceptable, and accountable mental health services are among the most urgent societal needs in the United States and in the rest of the world as well. What are the impacts of social justice issues on the treatment processes? How do we respond to these challenges as mental health professionals and citizens of the world?

NOTES

Danto, E. A. (2005). *Freud's Free Clinics: Psychoanalysis and Social Justice, 1918–1938.* New York: Columbia University Press.

Fonagy, P. (2003). Some complexities in the relationship of psychodynamic theory and practice. *Psychoanalytic Inquiry* 72(1): 13–47.

Gray, P. (2005). *The Ego and Analysis of Defense* (2nd ed.). New York: Jason Aronson.

Green, A. (2005). *Key Ideas for a Contemporary Psychoanalysis: Misrecognition and Recognition of the Unconscious.* New York: Routledge.

Mitchell, S. (2000). *Relationality: From Attachment to Intersubjectivity.* Hillsdale, NJ: The Analytic Press.

Shapiro, T. (2004). Use your words! *Journal of the American Psychoanalytic Association* 52(2): 331–53.

Stolorow, R. D. and G. E. Atwood. *Context of Being: The Intersubjective Foundations of Psychological Life.* Hillsdale, NJ: The Analytic Press.

Westen, D., and G. Gabbard (2002). Cognitive neuroscience and transference. *Journal of the American Psychoanalytic Association* 50(1): 99–134.

Stern, D. N. (2004). *The Present Moment in Psychotherapy and Everyday Life.* New York: W. W. Norton.

The International Perspective

Differences and Commonalities in
Psychoanalytic Theory and Practice

John S. Kafka

In a brief essay, I can only mention that there exist significant differences in the psychoanalytic climate and practice in different countries in which different psychoanalytic schools may be dominant. I cannot develop the theme of the prominent place of infantile sexuality in the theory and clinical work of some French analysts, for instance, or of the unhesitating and speedy transference interpretations of some British Kleinian analysts. But later I will consider the task facing analysts from different backgrounds when they work together in developing psychoanalytic institutes where there had never been psychoanalytic education, or where none had existed for a long time.

Some of the challenges that psychoanalysis encounters in the United States are global. These include the necessity to face the competition of quick, simplistic, narrowly symptom-oriented behavioral and biologic treatments. But the greatest challenges psychoanalysis faces are different in countries where it was politically suppressed. In these traumatized societies struggling to come to terms with new freedoms—and with the hidden remaining power of the old autocratic institutions—the great demand for and the great expectations from psychoanalysis constitute other challenges.

WHERE AND WHEN DID AND DOES PSYCHOANALYSIS PROSPER?

Hartmann thought, mistakenly I believe, that psychoanalysis develops and functions best in an "average expectable environment." Actually, Vienna, during Freud's time, was an extraordinary center of social, political, and cultural change.

Different but at least equally radical social change provided fertile ground for the development of psychoanalysis when dictatorships collapsed in Latin

America and especially in Germany, where, after the end of the Nazi regime, we saw the development of the second largest psychoanalytic community in the world. A spectacular growth of psychoanalysis in Eastern Europe that began after the end of the cold war is another example, and one with which I am familiar, of a situation favorable to the development of psychoanalysis. East Europeans flocking to psychoanalysis were eager to be in a situation in which one could talk freely and escape from the basic insanity of idealogically distorted language.

During the last twenty years, I have worked with analysts engaged in the development of psychoanalysis in Eastern Europe. Since traditional training facilities were not available, we had to develop new ways of organizing psychoanalytic education. In our evaluations, we emphasized competence and analytic sensitivity rather than formal educational criteria. We also developed, for instance, "shuttle" analysis, a system of various models of periods of training analysis in the West when and where no local training analysts were available.

The growth of psychoanalysis in Eastern Europe continues at a rapid pace. Fully recognized psychoanalytic societies and institutes, or provisional societies, or study groups, function in Budapest, Hungary; Prague, Czech Republic; Warsaw, Poland; and Belgrade, Serbia; as well as Romania and Croatia. A special psychoanalytic development program exists for Turkey. The Han Groen Prakken Institute for Eastern Europe (PIEE), a virtual psychoanalytic institute (it does not physically exist in any one location), organizes training and outreach activities in locations not yet ready for study group status.

There are two large study groups in Moscow. I currently chair the sponsoring committee developing these two study groups that will eventually become provisional and then full psychoanalytic institutes. Each of the members of this Moscow Sponsoring Committee comes from a different country. The committee members represent diverse psychoanalytic orientations. But they all face a task that differs from the psychoanalytic work and teaching that they do at home.

Eastern Europe has known recent massive social trauma. Our challenge consists of treating traumatized individuals in traumatized societies. Sometimes the interplay between social and individual trauma becomes especially vivid in Eastern Europe. A memorable example for me occurred in one psychoanalytic summer school when a French psychoanalyst presented a case and beautifully described subtle transference and countertransference fluctuations in the course of treatment. The discussant was an Ukranian psychiatrist who had started psychoanalytic training. He complimented the French analyst on this elegant and subtle presentation. He said, however, that most of his own patients had more simple transference feelings toward him. Few had grown up in an intact family. Many had grown up in institutions and considered Joseph Stalin their father. In transference, he said, he was either Stalin-devil or Stalin-god.

Psychoanalysis always involves the search for uncensored knowledge and self-knowledge. There is an underlying expectation in psychoanalytic thinking that such knowledge has a *therapeutic* function. Different psychoanalytic cultures, however, range from an almost exclusive focus on self-knowledge to a less exclusive one that gives more room to the therapeutic function of psychoanalysis. When teachers from such different cultures come together, they learn from each other and they have a joint learning experience when they meet the candidates who themselves had suffered severe personal and social trauma and who are treating patients whose personal and social traumas may have been even more severe. The issue of the differentially weighted emphases on self-knowledge enhancing or therapeutic functions in different psychoanalytic cultures, appears in a new light.

Autocratic regimes had attempted to entirely stifle the search for uncensored knowledge and self-knowledge. It is in working with traumatized individuals in traumatized societies that the consequences of the imposition of powerful strictures on thinking and self-exploration is particularly clear. The stifling of unhampered search for personal meaning and the forced immersion in ideologically crazy speech-making, does not just create interpersonal social difficulties, but also creates symptomatic pathological structures. Violence directed against others and/or oneself is just one of the symptomatic consequences of frozen thought. Here we can make a bridge to the challenge that psychoanalytic treatment faces in the West. As psychoanalysts, we see more clearly than other therapists the limits of only symptomatic treatment when it is divorced from the search for self-knowledge that is central to psychoanalysis.

Freud, ca. 1930, Max Halberstadt
Courtesy of Multiart.

11

The Application of Psychoanalysis in Nonclinical Domains

Stanley R. Palombo

FREUD'S VIEW OF THE UNIVERSE

An application of psychoanalysis is usually taken to mean a one-way transfer of conceptual tools developed by psychoanalysis into other problem areas. We all know of important psychoanalytic successes of this kind that have deepened our understanding of the arts and of all social and familial situations where individual motives have major effects.

Here, I will focus on a broader sort of application, Freud's influence on our larger views of nature and reality. This kind of application of psychoanalytic understanding is more of a two-way street. Freud's ideas on this subject continue to interact dynamically with a culture that has changed significantly since his time.

W. H. Auden wrote after Freud's death, now sixty-seven years ago:

> For one who lived among enemies so long;
> If he often was wrong and at times absurd,
> To us he is no more a person
> Now but a whole climate of opinion. (Auden, 1940a)

We are all aware that Freud made mistakes, but his mistakes were intelligently motivated. Freud had the rare capacity, like Aristotle, to say the best that could be said at the time about a subject and then moving on without a backward glance to something else. Neither Aristotle nor Freud never let the limitations of science or philosophy in their own day prevent them from generating novel ideas that helped them make sense of things. And both were willing to be wrong, unlike many of their more avid followers.

The climate of opinion that Freud created included a new understanding of human nature. Freud persuaded contemporaries like Auden that human feelings and actions are always more complex than they appear on the surface. How a person thinks or behaves is not a simple response to events of the moment but also to related events experienced at the deepest layers of his past history. Motives conflict, and those motives when actually expressed represent a compromise at best. Destructive wishes compete with feelings of love and affiliation and often overwhelm them. The political events surrounding Freud's death dramatized the terrible consequences of unchecked aggression. Civilization was hanging in the balance. Auden concluded in his great poem, "September 1, 1939" that "we must love one another or die" (Auden, 1940b).

The dangers of the undisciplined human psyche were certainly among Freud's major concerns, but his intellectual ambitions went beyond the understanding of human nature to the understanding of nature itself. Freud had an intuitive sense that what was true of human beings was true of the entire universe. This was not a popular view in Freud's time and is still unfamiliar to many today. The complexities of human life often appear antithetical to the simplicities and regularities of the physical world. Freud's view was that human life is a direct manifestation of an intrinsically complex universe.

His experience with psychoanalysis taught him that time is required to reveal the potential for adaptive organization inherent within the confusion of individual minds. Psychoanalysis was above all a process for generating new structure from existing materials. "Where Id was Ego shall be," he said famously. Freud sensed that reality was itself a process, but in his time it was difficult to conceptualize this intuition. The Neo-Darwinian view of evolution insisted that reality was just a series of unmotivated accidents.

Freud identified what he called two overarching instincts or principles. The life instinct was the tendency of things to come together to form more complex entities, a phenomenon we now call emergence. The death instinct was the tendency of complex entities to decompose into their constituents. Reality was a process in which these principles competed over time, just as the libidinal and aggressive instincts competed in the individual psyche. These ideas were not well received. It was not clear what kind of mechanism could produce the effects that Freud ascribed to his two principles.

Science has been catching up with Freud, however. It is now clear that nature produces increasingly complex organized systems at a rate much faster than can be accounted for by random events. The computer has proved to be an effective tool for simulating complex processes in which the cumulative effects of a long sequence of events may lead to abrupt and unpredictable change. A new understanding now exists about the role of time in fulfilling the potential for increasing organization in systems at all levels of complexity, from the nucleus of the atom to the nuclear family and the individual personality.

These new scientific ideas, which validate Freud's intuition, can help us understand the process of change in psychoanalytic treatment, as I have described it in my book, *The Emergent Ego* (1999). Contrary to popular misconception, science and psychoanalysis are as intertwined today as they were in Freud's time. The reputation of psychoanalysis in the contemporary world can only be improved if we continue to identify with Freud's determination to interact with the ideas that were continuing to evolve around him in science and in philosophy.

NOTES

Auden, W. H. "In Memory of Sigmund Freud." In. Auden, *Another Time*. New York: Random House, 1940a.

———. "September 1, 1939." In. Auden, *Another Time*. New York: Random House, 1940b.

Palombo, Stanley R. *The Emergent Ego: Complexity and Coevolution in the Psychoanalytic Process*. Madison, CT: International Universities Press, 1999.

Sublimation

Freud's Movement Outward toward Nonclinical Domains

J. David Miller

How does psychoanalysis move conceptually from the vast universe within our minds that Freud so brilliantly explored to the outer world of the "nonclinical domains?" Freud's concept of "ego" helps us to picture this pathway, since it mediates between the inside and the outside, most amazingly through the process of sublimation. This term refers to the way our unconscious wishes, fantasies, and conflicts not only impact the real world but shape whatever we create, for better or worse, in that world—relationships, works of art, scientific ideas, political systems, religions, or ideologies.

Freud first sketched out this concept over 100 years ago. In a 1905 paper on the theory of sexuality, he calls sublimation simply a "diversion of sexual instinctual forces from sexual aims and their direction to new ones (Freud, 1905, p. 178). His concept is so inclusive at this stage that it functions mostly as a placeholder. In the same paper he also calls sublimation "one of the origins of artistic activity," the basis of reaction formation, and the explanation for how "a person's 'character' is built up" (p. 238).

However, five years later, in his 1910 paper on Leonardo, Freud has worked out the concept of sublimation much more fully. He writes about how Leonardo sublimated his sexual desire for his mother. He says the artist redirected and transformed his desire to have her sexually into a desire just to look, and then more broadly, into an "urge to know" (p. 132) into curiosity, sexual and scientific. But Freud also says that a portion of Leonardo's libido was left unsublimated, remaining "fixated" on his mother, Caterina: "the blissful memories of his relations with her continued to be preserved in the unconscious" (p. 132). He says these memories "remained in an inactive state" but later resurfaced in his art: "what an artist creates provides at the same time an outlet for his sexual desire" (p. 132).

Leonardo found "an outlet for his sexual desire" toward his mother by painting not only the *Mona Lisa* but also the "series of mysterious pictures which are characterized by the enigmatic smile" (p. 134), according to Freud. He says that through sublimation Leonardo created displaced, symbolic representations of his earliest object: "the smiling women are nothing other than repetitions of his mother Caterina" (p. 111). In creating the portraits, Leonardo projected onto canvas an image of his mother, in fantasy and then in paint. If he could not have her in real life, unconsciously he would have her on canvas.

Thus it is with sublimation that Freud leads psychoanalysis into such nonclinical domains as art. Even if, to be whimsical, we define those domains concretely, as physical places, sublimation leads us, through the *Mona Lisa* and countless other works of art, to the Louvre. But not all sublimation is so ennobling. It also leads us from the Louvre, to *The Da Vinci Code*, and then on to the domain of Barnes & Noble and the Multiplex. These all reflect somebody's sublimation.

Despite its pervasiveness in our cultural life, my impression is that sublimation has not received the prominence it deserves in analytic scholarship. It seems to have slipped into the realm of ideas that are taken for granted and find little application. Perhaps this decline is due to a prevailing tendency to think of sublimation as Freud first defined it, as an over-inclusive, vague concept. To appreciate how Freud's theory of sublimation has evolved, in Freud's work and in the work of others, I recommend two comprehensive reviews, one by Heinz Hartmann (1955), and a more recent one, by Daniel Boesky (1986).

A few years after Boesky's review, in 1988, Hans Loewald published a monograph that integrates much post-Freudian thinking about the process. For Freud, Leonardo's aim was literally to recapture a visual image of a single person, his mother. For Loewald, the aim of sublimation is to recapture the subjective experience of the self in relationship to the mother. In a way, Loewald describes a two-person concept of sublimation. This view draws from Winnicott's work on what he calls "the location of cultural experience," the transitional space between fantasy and reality where mother and infant play creatively.

Freud, as we all know, anticipated many psychoanalytic concepts that he did not live long enough to develop. Among these, is Loewald's expansion of the theory of sublimation. In *The Ego and the Id* (*SE* 19:3-66), written 12 years after his Leonardo essay, Freud suggests that the ego "begins by changing sexual object-libido into narcissistic libido and then, perhaps goes on to give it another aim" (p. 30). In other words, Freud now implies that Leonardo painted portraits mirroring the image of his mother, perhaps, but certainly evoking a two-person experience, his internalized experience of being loved by her.

In his monograph on *Sublimation* (Loewald, 1988), which he wrote in haste, shortly before he died, Loewald, like Freud, touches on aspects that he never had time to explore. For example, he mentions the fate of the aggressive drives in sublimation, and its connection with "guilt, expiation, and atonement" (p. 82). These aspects still remain to be fully explored.

And so, one hundred years after he conceived it, Freud's idea of sublimation not only remains useful but continues to give rise to questions for further study. For those who are interested in the application of psychoanalysis to nonclinical domains, Freud is still very much with us.

NOTES

Boesky, Daniel (1986). "Questions About Sublimation," In *Psychoanalysis: The Science of Mental Conflict*. The Analytic Press, pp. 153–175.

Freud, S. (1905). *Three Essays on the Theory of Sexuality, SE* 7:125–245.

———. (1910). Leonardo da Vinci and a Memory of His Childhood, *SE* 11:59–137.

———. (1922). *The Ego and the Id, SE* 19:3–66.

Hartmann, Heinz (1955) Notes on the Theory of Sublimation, *Psychoanalytic Study of the Child* 10:9–29.

Loewald, Hans (1988). *Sublimation: Inquiries into Theoretical Psychoanalysis*. New Haven and London: Yale University Press.

Winnicott, D. W. (1967). "The Location of Cultural Experience," *International Journal of Psycho-Analysis*, 48:368–72.

The Application of Psychoanalysis in Nonclinical Domains

Jaine Darwin

Psychoanalysis in the twenty-first century has a pervasive influence outside of the consulting room. Psychoanalytic thought spans the globe, uniting us across countries and continents. We see the fingerprints of psychoanalytic thinking in the literature departments of universities and in the women's movement in the works of Judith Butler, Adrienne Rich, Dorothy Dinnerstein, Nancy Chodorow, Julia Kristeva, and Luce Irigaray among others.

Freud wrote psychobiographical studies, and we see this continued in the works of Erik Erikson, Robert Coles, John Mack, Frances Beaudry, and Vamik Volkan. In the theater or on the canvas, we appreciate and incorporate the intent of the artist viewed through a psychoanalytic lens. Could any of us look at the works of Eugene O'Neill or Edward Munch and forego the commenting as psychoanalysts about what the work tells us about the intrapsychic issues the creator is trying to master?

I will focus on psychoanalysis as a public health endeavor. In Freud's address to the Fifth International Psycho-Analytical Congress in Budapest in September 1918 he says,

> Now let us assume that by some kind of organization we succeeded in increasing our numbers to an extent sufficient for treating a considerable mass of the population. On the other hand, it is possible to foresee that at some time or other the conscience of society will awake and remind it that the poor man should have just as much right to assistance for his mind as he now has to the life-saving help offered by surgery; and that the neuroses threaten public health no less than tuberculosis, and can be left as little as the latter to the impotent care of individual members of the community. When this happens, institutions or outpatient clinics will be appointed, so that men who would otherwise give way to

drink, women who have nearly succumbed under their burden of privations, children for whom there is no choice between running wild or neurosis, may be made capable, by analysis, of resistance and of efficient work. Such treatments will be free. (Freud, 1918)

Psychoanalysis, as a public health discipline, responds to the pathogenic tendencies of our society through efforts at prevention. Wilhelm Reich amplified this by suggesting "to attack the neuroses by prevention rather than treatment." (Freud, 1918)

Anna Freud and Dorothy Burlingham did this with their Hampstead War Nursery, a center for young war victims established during World War II, saving hundreds of children from lasting trauma. They also used the nurseries as laboratories to first establish methods to best deal with children and then as sites to train teachers to utilize these principles. What began as a response to an emergency birthed a public health initiative to raise and educate psychologically healthy children.

Following the atrocities of 9/11, psychoanalysts in New York served the bereaved, the first responders, the rescue workers, and the school children to activate resilience and help them develop coping skills to bear the unbearable. These efforts are also serving as impetuses to train teachers to serve as the gatekeepers of children's mental health.

The pro bono program that I codirect, Strategic Outreach to Families of All Reservists (SOFAR) works with families and with soldiers deployed to Afghanistan and Iraq to provide support, psychoeducation, and treatment. Our mission is to prevent secondary trauma in the families, particularly the children. The families much prefer the support and psychoeducation that builds resilience and protects them from what they perceive as the stigma of seeking psychotherapy. Other analytic groups consult with judges in the courts to help them utilize psychoanalytic understanding as they impose sentences on the convicted felons. One analyst in Philadelphia works with the staffs of homeless shelters. By helping the staff to maximize their potential as caregivers, she indirectly contributes to reducing homelessness, a huge public health problem.

Both Peter Fonagy and Stuart Twemlow have written and lectured extensively to educators on ways to reduce violence in schools, a major public health problem. Ricardo Ainslie applies psychoanalytic principles to community interventions to deal with issues of race trauma. He worked with the residents of Jasper, Texas, after James Bird, the victim of a racial hate crime, was dragged to his death. Ainslie is now working with those convicted of the murder and their followers to understand the psychodynamics of the white supremacy movement and how community intervention can counteract their actions.

Psychoanalysis in addition to providing a way to clinically treat individuals also gives us a tool to improve and protect our society.

NOTES

Freud, S. (1918). Address to the Fifth International Psycho-Analytical Congress, Budapest, September 1918, in "Lines of Advance in Psycho-Analytic Therapy."

Playing, Creating, Learning

Katherine Brunkow

An amusing drawing of Sigmund Freud in tennis whites highlighted the *Wall Street Journal*, (August 11, 2006). Illustrator Ciardiello showed Freud with eyes on a bright yellow tennis ball, an analytic notebook in his back pocket, and a tennis racquet drawn back for a nice solid backhand. The article, "Working Out Your Anxiety," by Hannah Karp, described how Los Angeles tennis instructor Zach Kleiman uses the game of tennis to help his clients work on psychological issues. Discussion of his work included dynamics such as the persistence of conflicts around pleasing and competing with father, analyzing shots for hidden aggression and working through body issues and a mother's death.

Also in August 2006, a BBC radio program focused on problems in Creative Writing. One of the writing professors described the effectiveness of the technique of free writing for his students suffering from writer's block. He explained that this was based on what Freud had discovered about the usefulness of free association—that a seemingly foolish thought or sentence could lead through the mental process of association to something meaningful or even profound.

These two examples suggest familiar human struggles with inhibition that can interfere with the comfortable use of our energy, our bodies, and our creativity. Awareness of intrapsychic conflict in both examples shows how our lives and culture have been influenced by Freud's ideas, especially his understanding of the power of the Unconscious.

In my clinical practice as a psychoanalyst, I see daily evidence of people working through such conflicts that disrupt their lives and relationships. An example from outside the clinical domain comes from my work as a consultant to the Peace Corps. The organization's Office of Medical Services was faced with an important educational challenge. Peace Corps volunteers, new to countries with a high incidence of AIDS, did not seem to be taking seriously what they were taught in training about their risk for HIV infection. There were sad stories of Peace Corps volunteers finding out they were HIV positive because they simply had not believed that the risks of sexual activity with promiscuous partners or partners afraid of testing could apply to them. What we concluded was that the current approach of providing basic health information and statistics was not challenging the volunteers' defenses of denial, counterphobic risk-taking, and youthful grandiosity.

In order to break through these defenses, the Peace Corps Medical Service decided to ask returned volunteers who had become HIV positive if any of them would be willing to tell their stories in a way that could be used in training. I was the off-camera interviewer for the project, a training video called "Come Back Healthy." Five bright, capable, young Americans spoke, in front of the camera, about their idealism, vulnerability, and illusions. They explored how loneliness, stress, alcohol use, and longing for human contact compromised their judgment.

That video changed the impact of health training. Peace Corps doctors and nurses told us their trainees sat riveted by the stories. At first, they did not believe that these engaging, competent people could make such errors in trust and judgment. Gradually they realized that the volunteers on the screen were people like all of us, making mistakes and becoming careless at times of vulnerability—in our psychoanalytic language: when their ego functions were compromised.

Without Freud's model of the ego and its functions and his influence on his daughter Anna's elaboration of the mechanisms of defense, our team might not have understood the problem in the same way. The trainees' defenses had to be challenged. In a more practical sense for me, the task of interviewing was facilitated by analytic training. It had helped me learn to wait and let a story unfold and to respect the emotional power of the specificity of an individual's experience. It was this emotional power that broke through the trainees' defenses, enabled their identification with the people on the screen, and allowed them to think differently about their own vulnerability.

These examples from sports, the arts, and health education show a few of the many ways that Sigmund Freud's ideas continue to inform us in our play, our creativity, and our learning. I think he would have enjoyed that illustrated fantasy of Sigmund Freud playing tennis. In the game of Western Civilization, where systems of thought are regularly defeated, Feud's ideas have kept the ball in play for over a century.

Cross-Fertilization between Psychoanalysis and the Visual Arts

César A. Alfonso

It is no accident that psychoanalysis flourished in Vienna in the early decades of the twentieth century amidst an explosion of innovative artistic movements. While Freud's contemporaries in Vienna—artists like Gustav Klimt, Oskar Kokoschka, and Egon Schiele—created powerfully emoting expressionistic paintings, other European artists such as Franz Marc and Wassily Kandinsky formally moved away from centuries of figurative art to give birth to abstract art (Selz 1957), renouncing form to emphasize emotional context and expression of affect. Freud, an avid collector of antiquities, formulated his metapsychological hypotheses at a time and place in the history of art that coincided with an exploration with abstraction and a drastic departure from artistic representational conventions.

Psychoanalysis was an influential cultural precursor of the abstract revolution among twentieth century European and American artists. Not only did Freud's theoretical constructs find their way into the field of aesthetics and the general public, but also, by creating the language of psychoanalysis, he provided a timely context to appreciate and understand non-figurative art (Alfonso and Eckardt 2005).

The etymological root of the word "abstraction" from Latin means "to draw away from, to separate". Abstract art renounces form to express essence. Consider the following diary entry by the painter Franz Marc, dated Christmas 1914: "I am beginning more and more to see behind, or, to put it better, through things, to see behind them something which they conceal, for the most part cunningly, with their outward appearance by hoodwinking man with a façade which is quite different from what it actually covers" (Thoene 1938). Although abstraction goes into the making of any work of art—even a photographic depiction of nature allows for the artist's interpretation—abstract art that completely renounces representational form, dwells in the purely symbolic, on multiplicity of meaning, and clearly allows for the artistic expression of affect and of the artist's individuality.

Kandinsky, regarded by art historians as instrumental in propelling abstract art as the primordial movement of the twentieth century (Selz 1957), formulated in his writings the emphasis on content over form in nonfigurative art, giving color the power to express the artist's innermost feelings (Kandinsky 1947). Kandinsky spoke of an "internal necessity" expressed intuitively by painters by tapping into the unconscious to convert the language of emotions into color (Selz 1957).

As psychoanalysis established itself and evolved throughout Europe and the American continent, its cultural impact was prominent in the development of Surrealism in Europe, and later, abstract expressionism in the United States. André Breton (1969), the founder of Surrealism, and other artists such as Max Ernst, Joan Miró, Yves Tanguy, Salvador Dalí, and René Magritte, with their creative use of condensation, symbolization, transparency, sublimation, and juxtaposition, developed a pictorial style creating dream landscapes in imaginative primary process paintings. Surrealists tried to reconcile the abstract with the concrete (Whitfield 1992) with magical hyper-real images giving the viewer the experience of having a pictorial glimpse of the unconscious. One could also speculate that abstract expressionism, an artistic tradition born in the United States after World War II, was partly fueled by Freud's Vienna of the early 1900s. The abstract expressionists, including Jackson Pollock, Lee Krasner, Arshile Gorky, Willem de Kooning, and Mark Rothko, were a group of American artists who elaborated on Kandinsky's concept of internal necessity to completely forsake representation or resemblance to the world and give color and forceful brushstrokes central importance in the creation of a work of art. Abstract expressionists painted in primary process states directly pouring uncensored affect onto canvas. To quote the psychoanalytically informed observations of the historians H. W. Janson and A. F. Janson (1992): "[with Abstract Expressionism] painting became a counterpart to life itself, an ongoing process in which artists face comparable risks and overcome dilemmas confronting them through a series of conscious and unconscious decisions in response to both internal and external demands" (p. 438).

Freud's formulations—in particular the importance of the unconscious, psychic determinism, the concept of primary process, the technique of free association, and the interpretation of dreams—are an integral part of the cultural armamentarium of modern and contemporary artists, aesthetes, critics, and art historians. Psychoanalytic theory and technique became relevant to the development of artistic traditions in the twentieth century and psycho-analysis and aesthetics have been intertwined ever since in a journey of cross-fertilization.

NOTES

Alfonso, C., and Eckardt, M. H. (2005). Epilogue—Creativity and Polysemy—On the limits of pathography, psychobiography and art criticism. *Journal of the American Academy of Psychoanalysis* 33(1): 235–37.

Breton, A. (1969). *Manifesto of Surrealism*. Ann Arbor, MI: University of Michigan Press.

Janson, H. W., and Janson, A. F. (1992). *A Basic History of Art*. Prentice Hall Publishers, Englewood Cliffs, NJ: Prentice Hall.

Kandinsky, W. (1947). *Concerning the Spiritual in Art*. New York: Wittenborn, Schultz.

Selz, P. (1957). Aesthetic theories of Wassily Kandinsky and their relationship to the origin of non-objective painting. *The Art Bulletin* 39.

Thoene, P. (1938). *Modern German Art*. Middlesex, England: Pelican Books.

Whitfield, S. (1992). *Magritte*. London: South Bank Centre.

What Might Freud Say About the Coming Century?

Edith Kurzweil

Freud might begin: "Ladies and Gentlemen, after three score and four years, I am eager to hear about the novelties and improvements you have introduced into psychoanalysis since I last revised my Introductory Lectures."

He might well go on to state that he was delighted to find out that his creation, psychoanalysis, had been thriving, and had spread throughout Western civilization, although he might add that he was annoyed at being misquoted by people who hadn't bothered to read his works and was being blamed for things he never had said or thought. But I assume that he would highly approve of the many advances in theory and therapy—by those who have preserved "the gold of psychoanalysis," the unconscious—and would look askance at simplifications. His prediction that psychoanalytic thought would conquer the world had come true. But he might be as concerned about the movement—its organizations and endless splits—as he had been when Alfred Adler left in 1911 and Carl Jung soon thereafter.

As a sociologist who is looking at the place of psychoanalysis and its importance in the culture, I have found that people take from those portions of Freud's oeuvre that best suit their requirements—in line with their own culture's history and belief systems. For instance, German and Austrian therapists, sooner or later, deal with patients who are trying to come to terms with their own and/or their family's pasts during the Nazi period and are likely to model some of their clinical work on Alexander and Margarete Mitscherlich's *The Ability to Mourn* (1967). Their French colleagues, even those not in the footsteps of Jacques Lacan, are more concerned with the language of psychoanalysis than either their German- or English-speaking brethren. In America, psychotherapists are bound to live up to our cultural values of fairness—to women, homosexuals, minorities, and so on. Whether or not these issues are being introduced in therapeutic sessions, they are givens for both therapists and their patients. (I am using that term, because for the most part only potential candidates tend to undergo a classical psychoanalysis of four or five weekly sessions.)

Since I have only five minutes to talk, I will limit myself to two of Freud's points about culture.

1. His *Weltanschauung* (world view)
2. His insistence that psychoanalysis is a science

WELTANSCHAUUNG

Freud's *Weltanschauung* derived not only from his medical training and from his neurological research but from his broad background in Greek and Western philosophy, from having read Nietzsche and Schopenhauer as well as the German and English classics by the time he left his gymnasium—and from his fluency in English as well as in Greek and Latin. The persons who joined his circle—whether physicians or not—shared these experiences or soon caught up. I dare say that today's therapists do not dispose over such an intellectual range.

Freud criticized all *Weltanschauungen* from this broad perspective, as "intellectual constructions that solve all problems of our existence on the basis of one overriding hypothesis, that leaves no question unanswered, and in which everything that interests us finds its fixed place."[1] In 1917, he stated that believing in the future of Marxism, or in religion—whether Christianity, Judaism, or Islam—"can make one feel secure in life, know what to strive for, and how to deal with one's emotions and interests." And he maintained that "psychoanalysis, [unlike Marx's writings that have taken the place of the Bible and the Koran as a source of revelation], is incapable of creating a *Weltanschuung* of its own, but that it does not need one, because it is part of science and can adhere to the scientific *Weltanschuung*.[2]

PSYCHOANALYSIS IS A SCIENCE

We have come a long way since then. Now that the Marxist experiment has failed, do more and more psychoanalysts revert to believing in the Bible and the Koran? And are American therapists able to avoid approaching all issues from the perspective of diversity—in which psychoanalysts themselves believe? Does that mean that they must support the current cultural values by dichotomizing—one religion against another, one political party against another, or one candidate against another, and so on? Freud, I believe, managed to avoid such traps by emphasizing that psychoanalysis was a *science*. He managed to rise above the cultural illusions of his time by searching for the truth underlying the prevalent assumptions.

This is more difficult now that psychoanalysis is ubiquitous, and that its institutes are integrated; that an elaborate system of reimbursement has been put in place with much difficulty; that an egalitarian ethos was established after the psychological institutes whose members had had less rigorous training than those who belonged to the IPA and the APA won their lawsuit a few years ago. Now that most well-regarded psychoanalytic institutes have been recognized, could their members really afford to rock the boat?

Freud, who came upon the importance of the unconscious in the course of his neurological research, always insisted on its scientism and, in 1915, postulated that: *"for the present . . .* [psychology must] proceed according to its own requirements," and went on to add that: "after we have completed our psychoanalytic work we shall have to find a point of contact with biology."

By 1920, he stated that biology was "the land of unlimited possibilities" and that in a few dozen years its answers may well "blow away the whole of our artificial structure of hypotheses."[3] Up to a point, this already is happening. Many persons now seek help from pharmacologists rather than therapists. And we regularly read about new medications. Recently, for instance, we learned that a pill to relieve stuttering is in the works.

In 1932, Freud noted:

> No reader of an account of astronomy will feel disappointed and contemptuous of the science if he is shown the frontiers at which our knowledge of the universe melts into haziness. Only in psychology is it otherwise. . . . What people seem to demand of psychology is not progress in knowledge, but satisfactions of some other sort.[4]

In the interim, this search for satisfaction has multiplied exponentially, as modern culture continues to offer more and more consumer goods and promises not just the conditions for happiness but happiness itself.

Although it probably will be a long time before neuroscientists such as Mark Solms have pinpointed the exact locations of patients' emotions that they may experience in therapeutic sessions, this indicates that the current focus of psychoanalysis is shifting. As you know, a number of neuroscientists already are cooperating with psychoanalysts who are becoming knowledgeable in the neurosciences and in biology and physiology.

If this is to be the way of the future, medically trained therapists will have an easier time than those with a background in psychology and social work.

This is bound to go against the grain of our culture's belief in fairness—by inadvertently creating a new elite. Will that bring us full circle back to earlier times? If so, you may well want to contemplate training aspiring therapists both more broadly and more scientifically. This is a difficult question that you may well want to address at some point.

NOTES

1. S. Freud, *SE*, 22, *The Question of a Weltanschauung*, p. 158.
2. S. Freud. *New Introductory Lectures on Psycho-Analysis*. New York: Norton, 1965.
3. Mark Solms and Oliver Turnbull. *The Brain and the Inner World*. New York: Other Press, 2002, p. 298.
4. Op. cit. Preface.

12

A Brief Introduction to the Current Significance of Freud's Models of the Mind

K. Lynne Moritz

In this section, two panels present essays on psychoanalysis as cultural theory. How has psychoanalysis entered into our culture? How has it become a part of us and a part of the way we think and organize our understanding of our world?

This first panel addresses Freud's model of the mind—or shall we say, his models of the mind. I assume we are addressing the significance for modern life of Freud's topographic and tripartite models. One does not replace the other—rather, the two models account for different aspects of the mind—like wave theory and particle theory for different aspects of how light behaves.

The topographic model—the Systems Unconscious, Preconscious, and Conscious—was developed in relation to Freud's *Interpretation of Dreams*, around 1900, and was used to explain the clinical fact of the forgetting of dreams, slips of the tongue, and the vicissitudes of repression. This model describes mental content according to its accessibility to consciousness. Nowadays, the essentials of this model have become so much a part of our way of experiencing modern life that, in general, no thought is given to it—a human unconscious is assumed. The public takes as truth the clinical experience that unconscious motives affect our behavior, that irrational forces determine far more of our attitudes and actions than we are aware. All of us search for root causes, we examine child-rearing practices, we ask about traumatic events when behaviors occur that seem incomprehensible. At least these tenets of the Freudian models of the mind are assumed for *others*—though they may go long unrecognized in the self.

But, as Freud soon realized, the topographic model does not account for other aspects of mental life—what about anxiety dreams? Punishment

Freud, 1932
Courtesy of Multiart.

dreams? Why would one falsely confess to a heinous murder? Why do people doggedly repeat actions that experience proves will bring them only pain or humiliation? Why are we sometimes doomed to choose new versions of the same unhappy relationship? Freud did not return to model building for some years. Then in 1923, he brought forward the tripartite model, developed to account for these and other psychological phenomena. Thus, ego, id, and superego also entered the vocabulary of the popular imagination. Conflict theory lives!

As the explanatory power of these models for human behavior and neurotic illness became widely recognized and assimilated, especially after the success of psychoanalytic perspectives to assist soldiers in World War II, other innovators built on portions of the theory and began what has become a massive proliferation of derivative psychotherapies. Freud's models are also the stepping off point for other models of the mind within psychoanalysis — dyadic models rather than the familiar intrapsychic one. These modifications and extensions, however, are all deeply rooted in Freud's fundamental insights into the structuring of mental contents and the clinical demonstration that the mind can be influenced by a "talking cure." Our current concepts of the importance of child rearing techniques, the ubiquity of transference, trauma and cumulative trauma, repression, attachment, mentalization — all owe their fundamental assumptions to Freud's work. Indeed, the research is well known to us that shows that even the much researched cognitive behavioral therapy achieves better results the more closely it resembles psychoanalytic psychotherapy.

Yet forces are also afoot that counter an appreciation of Freud's work. For one, the very popularization of Freud's insights has diluted and distorted understanding of the actual theory even among psychotherapists. Furthermore, market factors as well as the frantic pace of our new age have come to favor the "quick fix" over therapies that require time for more basic change. Even more potent has been the market control exerted by the medical-industrial complex, including managed care, the pharmaceutical industry, and biological psychiatry, partly supported by the multitude of textbooks of psychology and by generations of academics who have been raised to bash Freud — often without challenge. Much work remains to reopen the doors that these forces seek to close to psychoanalysis, both as a treatment method and as a theory of the mind. Fortunately, in the last ten years we have found ourselves at a new renaissance. Not only has research in cognitive psychology and neuroscience dramatically converged with psychoanalytic science, supporting and underpinning many of the most fundamental of Freud's hypotheses, but psychoanalysis has found its way into the humanities departments in many of our universities. We find that psychoanalysis is at the cutting edge of new research in the social sciences as well as in neuroscience.

What remains true is the dramatic explanatory power of Freud's theory of the mind. It is our challenge to bring these understandings to each new generation in an increasingly complex and over-stimulated world. As a consultant to the American Psychoanalytic Association proposed, imagine the world if the 10,000 best minds in each generation of college students could be exposed to the thrill of the insights of psychoanalysis! It is our challenge to make that happen.

Freud's 150th birthday and the Austrian Embassy here in Washington have given us this opportunity to turn outward and to remind the world of the rich legacy of Freud's genius.

Reflections on the Relevance of Sigmund Freud's Ideas for Modern Society

Usha Tummala-Narra

In reflecting on the relevance of Sigmund Freud's model of the human mind to contemporary times, one of the things that stands out for me is Freud's own study of culture, history, archeology, and anthropology of ancient Western civilizations from which he derived some of his understanding of the individual as in conflict with larger society and culture (Freud, 1930). His aim was to establish a discipline of psychoanalysis that was based on modernist and positivistic ideals. At the same time, Freud's development of psychoanalysis as theory and technique was never divorced from cultural experience and political realities. Freud's ideas developed in a pre– and post–World War II European context where he and his family faced persecution in the latter part of his life.

In considering certain components of Freud's model of the mind, such as his psychosexual theory, it can certainly be argued that his ideas are gender and culturally biased. At the same time, there is a ubiquitous quality to Freud's ideas, such that those of us who identify with cultural contexts that are far different in some important ways from those of Freud and European and North American contexts, are still compelled by his ideas of human nature. Freud's ideas extended to a wide audience of intellectuals, even as far as Calcutta, India, the home of the first Indian psychoanalyst, Girindrashekhar Bose. By 1914, Bose had developed his psychoanalytic ideas almost independently of Freud and published a book entitled *Concept of Repression* in 1921. A correspondence between Bose and Freud began in 1921 and lasted sixteen years (1921–1937); their letters indicate Freud's ambivalence about addressing the cultural specifics of Bose's ideas, particularly in light of Freud's identifications with European intellectual traditions and Bose's identifications with Indian cultural ideology and spirituality (Akhtar and Tummala-Narra, 2005). While postindependence India experienced a decline in psychoanalysis, largely because of poverty, war, and partition, Freud's and Bose's ideas resurfaced in the past twenty-five years within a diaspora of psychoanalysts of Indian origin which spans India, England, the United States, Canada, and Australia.

In my own professional work, I have wondered at times what it may mean for an Indian American female psychologist to be so interested in the theories of the mind developed by a male Viennese psychiatrist in the early twentieth century. What I have found is that clinically, his ideas allow for a better understanding of long standing complicated human struggles and character issues. His notions of the symbolic, evident in his dream theory, challenge us to consider the workings of the unconscious mind. Freud challenged us to examine traditional conceptualizations of culture and religion and to consider a world that is not free from human suffering. He did not see the individual's past or a society's past as something that can be eradicated or outgrown but as an integral part of his/her existence. These were revolutionary ideas.

Freud examined questions concerning the relationship between society and the individual and wondered what may happen if cultural factors fail to explain the individual's conflicts related to sexuality and aggression. To Freud, religion was an "illusion," an attempt to cope with fear and longings (Simmonds, 2006). While he dismissed the potential for positive and adaptive aspects of religious faith, it is interesting to speculate how his theory may be applicable to present day political and religious tensions within and across nations, particularly with the rise of fundamentalism across different political and religious contexts.

The study of the unconscious has extended into the study of social phenomenology, including racism, sexism, and homophobia. Contemporary issues such as immigration, globalization of world economies, and the role of the Internet can be understood from Freud's view of society as impinging on the individual, as these changes offer, paradoxically, new material possibilities for individuals in the face of emotional disconnection and loss. Increasing pluralism in our society is reflected in the diversification of psychoanalysis itself and the varied extensions of Freud's theories of the human mind in the work of object relations, self-psychological, and relational psychoanalysts. These developments speak to both necessary reformulation of Freud's ideas in the practice of psychoanalytic work and the potential for broadened applicability of Freud's model of the mind in the future. This sentiment can be heard in Freud's statement, in his paper on Family Romances (Freud, 1908). "Indeed, the whole progress of society rests upon the opposition between successive generations" (p. 298).

NOTES

Akhtar, S., and Tummala-Narra, P. (2005). Psychoanalysis in India. In S. Akhtar (ed.), *Freud along the Ganges: Psychoanalytic reflections on the people and culture of India* (pp. 3–25). New York: Other Press.

Bose, G. (1921). *Concept of repression*. Calcutta: Sri Gouranga Press.

Freud, S. Family Romances (1908). In P. Gay (ed.), *The Freud reader*, 1989, (pp. 297–300). New York: W.W. Norton & Company.

Freud, Sigmund. *Civilization and Its Discontents*. New York: W. W. Norton; reissue edition, July 1989. (Originally published in 1930 in German as *Das Unbehagen in der Kultur* [The Uneasiness in Culture].)

Simmonds, J. G. "Freud and the American physician's religious experience." *Mental Health, Religion & Culture* 9(4) (September 2006): 401–5.

Fear of the Devil Within

Miriam Pierce

Pondering the question of cultural theory and Freud's model of the mind, what came to my mind was the case of a former patient; a young Latin American woman seeking a successful career as an artist, living on her own in New York City in a neighborhood that embodied the ethnic and cultural diversity of this modern-day city. She worked and studied with a group of artists who, like her, came from other countries and who, in the main, lived as struggling students. Like Frida Kahlo, the Mexican artist whose father was European and mother was Mexican, my patient explored her diverse heritage through her creative art. She was very interested in her own internal turmoil as well as the political turmoil within both her family and in her country's history in dealing with the "primitive" native and colonial European heritage.

My patient came for help because, following the recent breakup of a long-term relationship with a boyfriend, she was suffering from panic attacks, an inability to sleep, and intensive homophobic fears. She was in her mid-twenties and had not had any lesbian concerns until the breakup. While she had friends who were gay, she had never felt interested in sexual relationships with women, and the thought felt alien to her. I believed that the intensity of the anxiety she experienced indicated that these fears had exposed underlying identity concerns that had not been dealt with during her childhood and adolescence.

Her Latin American maternal grandmother had married a European businessman and thus the family spanned two cultural worlds. Her parents were divorced when she was three years old, and since her mother worked long hours, she spent a good part of her childhood in her maternal grandparents' home. She had visited with her birth father during summer holidays but had a distant relationship with him during her childhood. Now when she visited her family she stayed with her maternal grandparents. The short clinical vignette that follows takes place after a six-week trip to visit her family in Latin America. In her family, women are expected to marry in their early twenties. They would question her about her unmarried status and disapproved of her lifestyle in New York. Prior to her leave taking, she worked in therapy to prepare and fortify herself for the reunion and the anticipated criticism.

In the first session following her family visit, she reported that she had been able to experience a rapprochement with her mother. While she found her mother physically distant and nonnurturing, she was nevertheless able to appreciate her mother's intelligence while recognizing her emotional limitations. This ability to see her mother through different "lenses" came about after an experience in which she had participated with her artist friends. In her country there is a drug practice that purports to offer a mind-expanding and mind-cleansing opportunity, the native equivalent of a growth experience. She had previously been reluctant to participate, but this time felt compelled to do so by her friends.

The participants sat in a circle with a shaman at the center beating a drum while the drug was given. He chanted a rhythm, which seemed to move from his belly upwards. This drug and the accompanying rhythm appeared to induce vomiting on cue, while the participants were mesmerized by the chanting. My patient felt as though she was experiencing her own birth, which was violent at first and gradually became less so but was nevertheless a primal, primitive experience. Then, as in a dream, she felt she was being chased by a devil-like figure, but when she turned to look she identified the attacker as herself.

Upon her return, in the reunion with me she was relieved to be able to recapture the sense of constancy that we had established before she left for this extended break. She noted that she had felt at the time that she could recover from her drug-induced hallucinatory experience by keeping me in mind, knowing that she would be returning soon to our sessions. We approached this material as we would a dream, my patient associating to the images and her affective responses. While proceeding with our analytic work, I kept in mind Freud's tripartite model of the mind, as elaborated in "The Ego and the Id." This model informed the primitive psychic world that my patient was frightened of and alone in. Volume 19 of the *Standard Edition* not only begins with "The Ego and the Id," it also contains articles that explore a seventeenth-century demonological neurosis, a possession by the devil. Freud discusses the psychological meaning of the pact with the devil as a way of overcoming a sense of powerlessness. My patient recognized the attacker demon within herself; working with me provided the background of safety she needed to allow herself to explore these persecutory anxieties.

I understood the attacker in her dream state as the primitive aspect of her superego. She had made a pact with the "demon devil" aspect of her id. This was revealed during the course of her treatment as material surfaced that had not been not heretofore revealed. Her self-reflecting ego capacities gave her a new perspective, and the therapeutic alliance allowed her to explore deeper and earlier trauma, thus alleviating the intensity of her anxiety and guilt.

Freud's tripartite model of the mind informed the clinical work with my patient—a young modern woman living in a modern world, bridging the cultures in which she was raised—and, I believe, it continues to be a relevant model for our practices in the twenty-first century.

NOTES

Freud, S. (1923). The Ego and the Id. *SE* 19:13–56.
——. (1923). A Seventeenth Century Demonological Neurosis. *SE* 19:73–105.

Freud's Model

The I and the It

L. Gordon Kirschner

Early in his work with Breuer, Freud saw that hidden thoughts controlled the behavior of his patients. When the thoughts were revealed the behavior changed. Freud proposed a model in which the mind was divided into three parts: the conscious that one is aware of, the preconscious, containing latent thoughts that could readily be brought forth, and an unconscious, where thoughts were actively repressed and could not be made conscious unless the dynamic force of repression was overcome. He developed psychoanalysis as a technique to access repressed thoughts, to bring them to consciousness, thus enabling the patient to deal with them. Conflict in the mind was conceived as the motivation for repression and conscious awareness was to be the means to enable resolution of the conflict. Early on, he proposed that instinct was a blind force opposed by social demands.

In 1923 Freud published "Das Ich und das Es" (The Ego and the Id) in which he proposed a new division of mind in three parts, the third now being the Uber Ich.[1] We are all familiar with these terms in their Greek translation as the ego, the id, and the superego. They might better be translated into English as the I, the It and the Over I. Bruno Bettelheim argued that even the ordinary English words fail to carry the rich meaning of the original, saying: "During their early years, all Germans have the experience of being referred to by means of the neuter pronoun *es*."[2] This three part division of mind signaled that the "I" was an outgrowth of the "It" and in part remained unconscious, in intimate contact with the irrational, selfish, infantile regions of mental life. The "Uber Ich," or superego was recognized as an accretion of memories of guidance, both benign and malignant, of experiences of danger and survival. These memories may be preconscious or unconscious, and influence the working of the "I."

Now we know that people are moved by perceptions and ideas that they are unaware of. Science demonstrates that our brains comprise functional units that must work together and that some of the time they fail to do so. We now know that the memory is a set of varied functions, some conscious and some not. Conditioned fear operates entirely out of awareness. Implicit, procedural memory, guides us through performance we can only explain indirectly. Implicit memory biases our expectations. Explicit memory is our conscious guide. We talk more now of the self, rather than of "I" or ego. This self is a construct at the center of our mental organization, a process instead of a thing, which coordinates the mind's various functions through the unifying effect of conscious awareness.[3]

Recognizing that the brain is the most complex system that we know of, Stanley Palombo has applied Kaufman's theories of self-organization to show that order emerges naturally and that the psychoanalytic process can reveal that order, and promote reordering to the lasting benefit of the patient.[4] We seek further understanding of integration of the functional and anatomical units of the brain and continue to believe that disintegration of mental functions is the basis of psychopathology.[5] We continue to rely on the conception of mind as comprised of separate, functional systems within a larger system. The idea of unconscious motivation is relied on throughout our society today. Unfortunately, this insight has not yet been put to full use for the greater good; rather, it is relied on daily in strategies to manipulate and influence us all.

NOTES

1. Freud, Sigmund. "The Ego and the Id." *SE*, 19, 3–63.

2. Bettelheim, Bruno. *Freud and Man's Soul*, pp. 53–55. New York: Alfred A. Knopf, 1983.

3. LeDoux, Joseph, Jacek Debiec, and Henry Moss. "The Self, From Soul to Brain," *Annals of the New York Academy of Sciences*, V. 1001. New York, 2003.

4. Palombo, Stanley R. *The Emergent Ego, Complexity and Coevolution in the Psychoanalytic Process*. Madison, CT: International Universities Press, 1999.

5. Siegel, Daniel J. *The Developing Mind*. New York and London: Guilford, 1999.

The Brutality of the Death Instinct in Our Modern Troubled Times

James Kleiger

Open your paper almost any morning and look for the article that tells about the latest round of killings in Iraq or Afghanistan. One cannot miss the stories about the daily suicide bombings, the mounting toll of death and destruction in Afghanistan, Iraq, Lebanon, or Israel; the drumbeat of a body count and number of maimed American service personnel. We read and hear about accusations of untruths and outright lies from the highest levels of national leadership. How ironic that in 1915, Freud, in a lecture at the University of Vienna, would ask his audience to "think of the excesses of brutality, cruelty, and mendacity, which is now allowed to spread itself over the civilized world" and to admit that evil cannot be excluded from basic human nature. Peter Gay pointed out how the "great slaughter" between 1914 and 1918 with its stark truths about human savagery revealed in combat and in bellicose editorials played a significant role in forcing Freud to assign enhanced status to aggression.

There were, of course, other factors besides World War I that led Freud to posit a second primary drive, and ultimately the death instinct. Death surrounded Freud, not just from the war in Europe but in his personal life that was saturated with the deaths of some of his closest friends and family members, most especially, his daughter Sophia.

In our current times, we, as a society, are also not only immersed in a war of unspeakable brutality, but we, too, share a collective grief for the loss of so many innocent lives and for a loss of our own innocence as a society, as well.

In *Beyond the Pleasure Principle*, Freud wrote about how the pleasure principle could no longer account for all mental acts. In addition to the repetition compulsion and transference resistance, Freud posited the existence of the death instinct as the ultimate regressive process whereby all life seeks to return to its earlier nonorganic state. In essence, he spoke about a primary masochism in which each organism sought to self-destruct and return to an earlier form. In a startling reversal of earlier held positions, Freud moved the Nirvana Principle, long synonymous with the pleasure principle, into the camp of his new death instinct. In essence, the Nirvana Principle was now thought to regulate the death instinct, as if the ultimate search for constancy is in death.

Generations of analysts rejected Freud's more speculative theorizing about the inherent drive toward states of nonexistence, while most had little difficulty accepting the innateness of humankind's aggression toward one another.

We have examples of both manifestations of Thanatos these days. As an innate force projected outward onto others, sadistic and destructive acts of sectarian violence have been committed. Whether committed by Hutu or Tutsi; Serb or Croat; Shiite or Sunni, we live in a time replete with atrocities. The extent of unbridled sadism is numbing. This is what Freud must have experienced in the wake of the violent conflict that swept Europe.

Yet we have also encountered the other form of Thanatos, the less popular kind, originally referred to as the "silent death instinct." If, according to Freud's controversial theory, the ultimate goal of existence is to return to an inorganic state, then suicide would certainly further the process. The cult of the suicide bomber can be understood from multiple vantage points— politically, historically, culturally, and spiritually. However, trying to achieve a modicum of understanding of this unfathomable issue from a psychoanalytic perspective may provide an additional bit of insight to make that which is incomprehensible somewhat more comprehensible.

By reassigning the Nirvana Principle to the camp of Thanatos, Freud introduced an erotic and subtle pleasurable element into the death instinct. Thus, there is a blurring of drive derivatives between those of Eros and those of Thanatos in the act of a suicide bombing. Centuries ago, the Roman philosopher Seneca, before he committed what was considered a noble suicide, spoke of the glorification of death and used the phrase the "lust for dying."

Suicide bombings would seem to bridge the gap between sadism and masochism, homicide and suicide, and in some way, Thanatos and Eros. In taking one's life by strapping a bomb around one's waist, the goal certainly is to externalize as much destructiveness as possible. In doing so, the bomber, himself or herself, is the first to be destroyed by their own hand. However, while the ultimate purpose of the silent death instinct is to return to a state of nothingness, for the suicide bomber, the ultimate goal is to achieve a higher form of life after death, martyrdom with the promise of erotic paradise. Some have even noted that the moment of blowing oneself up is the ultimate anticipation of pleasure.

13

Psychoanalysis and Society

Can Psychoanalysis Help Us Understand Modern Conflicts?

Richard Ruth

Historically and conceptually, it is difficult to imagine politics before Freud. His discovery that unconscious, conflictual, and lawful mental representations underlie, and differ from, external expressions is necessary to political analysis. But how to understand the pathways by which the personal comes to affect the social and political? The title of this chapter offers an intriguing clue — "modern conflicts" can be read in a clinical, or a sociopolitical, context.

A patient came to see me several years ago. Like me, he was Argentine. He had been raped while in political detention, and from this had acquired AIDS. After his diagnosis, he decided to come to the United States. He was concerned that, as his health declined, he would be vulnerable, and that, had he stayed in Argentina, he might have inadvertently exposed, and endangered, his political connections and associations. To avoid this, he chose to die far from home. To his thinking, psychoanalysis was his only way to survive with integrity. He wanted to explore his experiences, their determinants and resonances, with space and fullness, and with an analytic listener. It was a courageous act, from which much understanding unfolded.

Perhaps it is not often framed this way, but one of Freud's contributions was that private stories in some circumstances demand to become part of public discourse. Discourse then shapes thinking, and, from there, behavior — not in the linear pathway of stimulus and response, but in the more intricate process through which the unconscious becomes known and considered, and illuminates choice.

Courage becomes transformative, and meaning emerges, when ideas find expression in grounded action. But action can feel elusive in psychoanalysis,

Freud with Sons in Uniform, Ernst and Martin, 1916
Courtesy of Multiart.

which insists on reflective space, the controversial stance of abstinence, a particular kind of diffuse attention and elongated time. Perhaps psychoanalytic thinking, especially on the sociopolitical level, and psychoanalytic practice, are best considered as kinds of crucibles, or incubators, in which the action of meaning-making takes place.

When Freud discussed his views on homosexuality, his text had a remarkably open weave. On one level, he was taking a welcome position; on another, he was modeling engagement with thinking about a charged topic, thoughtfully, carefully, deeply, and unflinchingly. He did not form a political movement; if he engaged in advocacy, perhaps it was the kind of curious analytic advocacy in which we are engaged here today. Was his writing transformative? I believe it was.

I got married last month, in Toronto, to my male partner—some seventy years after Freud's *Letter to an American Mother*. It was a joyous occasion, resonating deeply with what we analysts call "the good hour." But the good hour comes only after painstaking work, and working through. It can take analytic ideas a long time to develop, and to exert their full power.

I felt very close to Freud, that day in Toronto, and I give him credit for initiating what I came to experience as both culmination and beginning. Had Freud lived into our time, I suspect his radical curiosity, profound commitment to scientific discovery, and insistence that the job of theory is to point the way toward transformative practice would have led him to take great pleasure in our incremental social and political advances. And to look at us critically, in his stern way, when we imagined our society might settle for anything less.

Freud left us with open questions: How are personal and social conflict, and personal and social change, the same and different? Is analytic theory culture-bound and class-bound? Do analytic methods, or only analytic ideas, deserve to enter the social and political realms? He also left us a method to help answer our questions. It is a remarkable legacy that has transformed the world, and, in its evolution and action, is fully alive.

Psychoanalysis and Society

Can Psychoanalysis Help Us Understand Modern Conflicts? A Social Worker Speaks

Audrey Thayer Walker

"Can Psychoanalysis Help Us Understand Modern Conflicts?" A case vignette may well be a window into this exploration. A guiding principle of social work training is "start where your client is." So here we are in Washington, D.C., the anniversary week of 9/11! Five years ago on 9/11, at about 9:25 a.m., I looked out of my office window. I remember seeing the streams of people leaving offices, silently and relentlessly headed home. I remember the smoke from the Pentagon across the Potomac, the waiting room radio blaring a shocked announcer's voice saying that the two hits (New York) had become three (the Pentagon) and that another plane had crashed in Pennsylvania, headed, supposedly, for the White House (a few blocks away from my office)!

Horror. Numbness. Fear. Rage. What are we going to "do"—We dare not think!!

Boundaries blurred: patients and therapists huddled together around the waiting room radio, immobilized, wanting to go home but frozen. People left—a psychiatrist was staying—the George Washington University Hospital emergency room, across the street, might need him. I had scheduled patients/clients all day. Interestingly, all kept their appointments.

Just like my clients, who have experienced extraordinary physical and psychological assaults and who disproportionately utilize their resources and energy for defensive purposes, so is society likely to do so. Can we face that our illusion of safety, mastery, and control in relation to the rest of the world, is just an illusion? What will take its place? What will be the future destructive reenactments? We in the psychoanalytic community know a great deal about such dynamics. Sometimes, in an attempt to resolve conflict, we unconsciously—preconsciously even—employ defensive psychic mechanisms that create that which we truly fear!

Our professions have taught us to ask questions. How did the United States get into a war in Iraq? How did the assault by those four planes become the United States attack on Afghanistan, Saddam Hussein, and Iraq and alienate the United States from most of the Middle East and from many of its allies? What were, and are, we thinking: what happened to our capacity to think and then speak that which we thought? Who are "we"—one amorphous whole, or many diverse subcultures, fractured, polarized, and/or unified? Where were (and are) the leaders? Who were they? Around whom did society organize? Psychoanalysis has taught us to talk, explore, think, and even speak. D.C.'s psychoanalyst, Justin Frank, author of the controversial, *Bush on the Couch* (Frank, 2004), shared publicly his thoughts, informed by his psychoanalytic training and experience. Otto Kernberg (1998) developed his paper referencing the narcissistic and/or pathologically narcissistic leader.

Freud also had some thoughts. He said history and context are important: who is doing what to whom under what circumstances? He understood man's capacity to regress to primitive states under pressure: He understood that members of a group could project wishes and disavowed aspects of themselves onto an idealized leader, regress, and allow that leader to think and/or act for them. He also knew the capacity of man's mind to intellectualize, to rationalize, and to think, the latter providing hope, and he knew that limits, structure, superego could be useful in channeling the primitive energy of affects into thinking, altruism, even sublimations. He understood that primitive affects push toward action, gratification, and that the tension between the impulse seeking gratification and civilization (the external and institutionalized superego representing limits for the supposed greater good) is necessary for survival and growth.

I have listed several of Freud papers that are relevant to today's topic:
"The Future of Illusion," 1927
"Civilization and Its Discontents," 1930
"Totem and Taboo," 1912, 1913
Group Psychology and the Analysis of the Ego, 1921

I am struck with the brilliance and insight of Freud's thoughts, especially within the context of his times and how these insights are so relevant to today. He wrote of hope (life) as well as destruction (death). No wonder my social work profession and my own Smith College School for Social Work found such grounding in psychoanalytic theory.

The United States is at war—a polarizing war! However, we in D.C. experienced the Pennsylvania plane that crashed on 9/11/01—the one where people came together, collaborated, and died, sooner rather than later, for the greater good—we experienced this as heroism. What would Freud say about this?

NOTES

Frank, J. A. (2004). *Bush on the Couch: Inside the Mind of the President.* New York: Regan Books.

Freud, S. (1913). Totem and Taboo: Some Points of Agreement between the Mental Lives of Savages and Neurotics. *SE* 13:vii–162.

———. (1921). Group Psychology and the Analysis of the Ego. *SE* 18:65–144.

———. (1927). The Future of an Illusion. *SE* 21:1–56.

———. (1930). Civilization and its Discontents. *SE* 21:57–146.

Kernberg, O. F. (1998). *Ideology, Conflict, and Leadership in Groups and Organizations.* New Haven, CT and London: Yale University Press.

Can Psychoanalysis Help Us Understand the Middle East Conflict?

Joseph P. Merlino

The application of psychoanalysis to world conflict typically takes the form of treating victims of war, aggression, and terror. However, it can also provide an understanding of those directly involved in such conflicts.[1] A most recent example is the Arab-Israeli conflict. In discussing the recent war, I repeatedly heard that the war seemed irrational. The consideration of anything "irrational" invokes the life and work of Sigmund Freud.

Freud helped the world realize that psychological reality is as real as objective reality—that forces that are unconscious are often more powerful than any of which we are fully aware. But does such knowledge help us understand something as studied as the battles of the Middle East?

Freud's genius was that his discovery of the unconscious mind and its mechanisms could be applied to help deepen knowledge of all areas of life including religion, culture, and history. Utilizing his approach to de-mystify the seemingly irrational goings-on in the Middle East requires the calm and unbiased study of the region's history and an appreciation of the very different worldviews of neighboring peoples fighting over a small parcel of land only 290 miles long by 85 miles wide.

Avner Falk, in his recent book, *Fratricide in the Holy Land*, notes, "The psychoanalytic view . . . focuses on the irrational aspects of the conflict—the unconscious role of the nation as mother, defensive group narcissism, historical hurts, narcissistic injury, denial, projection, splitting, externalization, and lack of empathy."[2] These are, of course, Freudian concepts as is the repetition compulsion[3] that can be seen operating in the Middle East. Here the Jews are seen as reliving the extermination of six million Jews between 1941 and 1945 while the Palestinian Arabs reexperience the handover of their land to Great Britain after World War I together with their defeat and humiliation during the war of 1948 in which hundreds of thousands of Palestinian Arabs lost their homes.

The conflicting nationalisms of the Jews and Arabs play a key role in the conflict with one side's victory leading to the other's shame and humiliation. Erik Erikson, who was analyzed by Freud's daughter Anna, described the process by which one group sees itself as human while seeing other groups as subhuman; one group is superior and immortal and the other group is inferior and inhuman. This *group narcissism* can be understood as a defensive mechanism against the low self-esteem resulting from its collective history of hurts, losses, and injuries.[4]

Freud, in his letter to Einstein, wrote that such conflicts "will only be prevented with certainty if mankind unites in setting up a central authority to which the right of giving judgment upon all conflicts of interest shall be handed over."[5] Freud believed in 1932, as seems true today, that "at the moment there seems very little prospect of this." Freud teaches us in *Why War?* his dual instinct theory in which there are those who seek to preserve and unite and those who seek to destroy and kill. He wrote that, "Anything that encourages the growth of emotional ties between men must operate against war." Freud likewise believed that whatever fostered the growth of culture worked against the making of war. Regrettably, the burden of evidence since Freud's time does not support this notion.[6] Recognizing that there are more followers than leaders, Freud envisaged a Utopian world in which the community of mankind "had subordinated their instinctual life to the dictatorship of reason."

Atkin writes, "I believe that a sociological-psychoanalytic study of the interaction at the interfaces of the organism and society is essential if we are to understand man both as the creator and the creature of his social institutions, the most destructive of which is war."[7] In other words, a psychoanalytic social psychology,[8] may contribute to a rational resolution of this conflict. The alternative is a repetition of the conflict with ever more deadly consequences.

LeBon recognized over a century ago, that "when masses become ideologized and politicized, they lose sight of the realities of the situation in which they are involved; they overestimate their strength . . . they are liable to gross error in assessing the strength of real enemies, [and] they imagine themselves to be all-powerful and experience a vast inflation of narcissistic feeling."[9] Through the mechanism of group regression, the crowd is able to trust the contradictory and absurd promises of their leader. Freud taught that only through the strength of the individual's ego can one prevail against such regression. However, Mitscherlich notes that even in the face of atrocities we are reluctant to intervene because we are either too selfish, or too splintered, or not willing to meddle in the affairs of a sovereign state.

Kohut optimistically believes that psychoanalysis can offer its deep insights about the individual to bear on group psychology in a sensitive and creative fashion so that in turn a decisive contribution can be made to the self-control of the group and its leaders. Kohut[10] sees the psychological task for man as withdrawing from the present search for external sources of pleasure and instead finding contentment from the enjoyment of values that are in harmony with our inner life. Freud is an outstanding example of such an inward shift.

NOTES

1. Cassimatis, E. G. (2002). Terrorism, Our World and Our Way of Life. *Journal of American Acad. Psa.* 30: 531–43.

2. Avner Falk. (2004). *Fratricide in the Holy Land: A Psychoanalytic View of the Arab-Israeli Conflict.* Madison: The University of Wisconsin Press, Terrace Books, p. 12.

3. Ibid., p. 18.

4. Ibid., p. 89.

5. Freud, S. (1932). *Why War? Collected Papers*, XXV, pp. 273–87. Heinz Kohut, *Self Psychology and the Humanities. Reflections on a New Psychoanalytic Approach*, edited and with an introduction by Charles B. Strozier. New York and London: W. W. Norton & Co., 1985.

6. Atkin, S. (1971). Notes on Motivations for War Toward a Psychoanalytic Social Psychology. *Psychoanalytic Quarterly* 40: 549–83.

7. Ibid.

8. Ibid.

9. Mitscherlich, A. (1978). Group Psychology and the Analysis of the Ego—A Lifetime Later. *Psychoanalytic Quarterly* 47: 1–23.

10. Kohut, H. (1973). Psychoanalysis in a Troubled World. *Annual Psychoanal*, 1: 3–25.

Can Psychoanalysis Help Us Understand Modern Conflicts?

William L. Granatir

Psychoanalysis is a psychology of the individual. The first to offer us a theory of personality from infancy to the development of a sense of self that freed us from former restrictions. He showed us a road map to help children develop into strong and independent adults. Studies of early infantile mother-child attachment has shown us the consequences of failure in such attachment. We now know that failure of attachment—early loss of love combined with neglect and insufficient emotional as well as physical nourishment—is a loss from which the child may never recover.

In my postretirement, in my volunteer work in the inner city schools of the District of Columbia, I saw that it did not take a great deal of clinical experience to notice the damage done to children by neglect and violence in the home and in the neighborhood. One sees the anxiety and depression of internalized loss and aggression and the restless, unruly, defiant children who are suspicious and untrusting of adults. Plagued by the surrounding violence and plagued by internal fantasies of aggression that interfere with attention, is it any wonder that so many children cannot learn to read? One result is that 35 percent of adults in the District of Columbia are unable to read beyond the third grade level. Thus they are unable to complete a simple legal document or to assist their children.

As psychoanalysts, we know a great deal about competition and conflict over difference on an individual level. We can provide education to a generation of children to help them prepare for parenthood and support to the self-respect of their children and their sense of equality with and respect for others.

The improvement in the civil rights of minorities and decrease in the prejudice toward them in the past fifty years was not assisted much by or our organizations (except as individual citizens). It is important to note that the

young men arrested recently in England for planning to bomb airplanes flying over the Atlantic were quoted in the press as feeling alienated from the society and humiliated by the prejudice against them as Muslims. Such senti-
ments have been expressed by some Arab-Americans of Muslim faith, and it
has been suggested that the humiliation and alienation they have experienced
has contributed to—if not caused—their susceptibility to recruitment into
groups advocating violence and terror.

Shame and feelings of humiliation have been experienced by most African-
American children. In my work with children in schools, as trust was developed in a relationship they all expressed feelings of shame about their poverty
and low status as African-Americans in our society. In a study of men in
prison in Massachusetts, James Gilligan (1966) found shame as an affect
prevalent in the men he interviewed.

I move to a related painful topic.

I am not alone in being reminded today of the 1930s and the proxy war in
Spain, as was the recent war in Lebanon between Hezbollah and Israel.

World War I began with the assassination of one man in Sarajevo. In the
most recent conflict in Lebanon, thousands have been killed and wounded. I
feel it is not inappropriate to bring up this subject in the Embassy of Austria,
a country friendly to the United States and one that has experienced its share
of warfare.

Recently, two men from Iran were interviewed on the *Jim Lehrer News
Hour*. They said, in an effort to explain the feelings and statements of their
president and leaders, that the Iranian people do not want to be "bullied" by
President George Bush—that they will not accept humiliation and that their
leaders insist on being treated with respect. If that is true, perhaps what Freud
termed the "soft words of reason may still be heard"; perhaps a dialogue is
still possible with Iranian and Syrian leaders. The sophistication of modern
weapons makes possible a degree of destruction worse than what took place
in World War II and worse than can be imagined.

In an exchange of letters with Albert Einstein at a time when war was
clearly imminent, Freud expressed despair about prevention of war. The war
to liberate Iraq and bring democracy to Iraq has not been convincing to any
Arab nation. It seems clear to them that the idea is prevalent that the United
States. is at war with the Muslim world. Just as clearly there are leaders and
many people in this country who are convinced that there are forces in the
Arab Muslim world dedicated to the destruction of the West.

Henry Kissinger, writing in the *Washington Post*, said:

> We are witnessing a carefully conceived assault. Not isolated terrorist attacks,
> on the International system of respect for sovereignty and territorial integrity.
> The creation of organizations such as Hezbollah and al-Qaeda symbolizes the

fact that trans-national loyalties are replacing national ones. The driving force behind this challenge is the jihadist conviction that it is the existing order that is illegitimate, not the Hezbollah and jihad method of fighting it. For the jihad adherents the battlefield cannot be defined by frontiers based on the world order they reject; what we call terror is, to the jihadists, an act of war to undermine illegitimate regimes. . . . Leaders therefore are torn between following principles of the international order, on which economies can depend, and yielding to (if not joining) the transnational movements on which their political survival may depend. . . . By the rules of the old international order, the war in Lebanon technically took place between two states—Lebanon and Israel—that in fact have very few conflicting interests. . . . By International rules the U.S. Secretary of State was obliged to negotiate with the Lebanese Government which controls no forces in a position to implement it while the only forces capable of doing so have never accepted it." Kissinger went on to say, "A common Atlantic policy backed by moderate Arab States must be a top priority, no matter how pessimistic previous experience with such projects leave one." (Kissinger, 2006)

I end my remarks in despair. The world is on fire. Our psychoanalytic insights are of little use in the face of the weakened position of the United Nations and the United States.

The United Nations does not have the forces to stop the genocide in Darfur as well as to monitor a cease-fire in the Middle East, where the determination by the president of Iran and the forces of Hezbollah and Hamas to destroy Israel has been expressed with self-righteousness or martyrdom and an indifference to human life

The United States is no longer the most powerful nation in the world. Weakened by the war in Iraq; having lost the respect of world leaders and of our allies in our ability to defend human rights; with an unprecedented national debt; and with the disapproval of the war in Iraq of about half of the people in this country, the United States is no longer the world leader. We are heading back to the Middle Ages—only this time with modern methods of destruction that can hardly be imagined.

NOTES

Gilligan, James. *Violence—Our Deadly Epidemic and Its Causes*. New York: Putnam & Sons, 1996.
Kissinger, Henry. *Washington Post*, September 13, 2006.

Freud's Contemporary Relevance

Nancy McWilliams

My immediate response to the question of whether psychoanalysis can help us to understand modern conflicts is that it is impossible for me to imagine understanding contemporary conflicts *without* psychoanalysis, without the legacy of Freud. Let me illustrate this by talking briefly about two different kinds of conflicts: those inside each of us and those between ourselves and others.

INTRAPSYCHIC CONFLICTS

Despite the universals in which we psychoanalysts are often fond of talking, cultures change, psychopathologies change, and individual psychologies change. There is always a tension between what changes and what remains continuous and unchanging. One of my favorite instances of significant change amid overall continuity concerns the observations of Martha Wolfenstein (1951) on "fun morality." When Freud's writings became popular in the United States and were assimilated into the utopian sensibilities of Americans, many well-intentioned people concluded, on the basis of Freud's observations about the neurotic suffering that attends severe self-criticism, that we should be reducing the harshness of children's superegos. Permissive preschools flourished, especially on the Upper West Side of Manhattan, and many families adopted a child-rearing ethos that eschewed criticism and encouraged children to "just have fun."

Wolfenstein discovered that the superegos of children in these environments were just as harsh as those of children reared under more traditional supervision, but that the *content* of those superegos was different. The children were just as prone to guilt as their traditionally reared peers, but what they felt guilty about was *not having enough fun*. They worried that they were disappointing their parents if they were not having a good enough time.

I doubt that Freud could have conceived of the current sheer velocity of technological and social change or fully envisioned the mass, consumeristic society we now inhabit. He may have seen it coming; he was fond of referring to the United States as "Dollarland." But that was a hundred years ago, before Madison Avenue had scarfed up his own ideas in the service of its agenda to increase our desires and offer lucrative material solutions to our most private conflicts. Could Freud have foreseen Fromm's (1947) "marketing personality"? Or Kohut's (1971) narcissist, devastated by covert shame and thwarted needs to idealize; or Kernberg's (1975) narcissist, dominated by envy and the need to spoil? Could he have imagined contemporary expressions of borderline dynamics—the relentless self-cutting, self-mutilating, vomiting, exercising? Several times in recent years I have heard case presentations of individuals who are "addicted" to their computers; they compensate for an abyss in their self-esteem by claiming false identities and having virtual love affairs with strangers in faraway countries while their families suffer from their distractedness and neglect.

Freud tended to assume a sense of agency, and he was keenly aware of the inevitability of grief, loss, and limitation. How could this man who emphasized the importance of compromising with painful realities have spoken with people raised, as are so many in this culture, with messages such as "You can be anything you want to be" and "You deserve only the best"? In purely descriptive terms, such messages border on the psychotic. How could he have functioned in a culture where limits are resented and denied, and pathological entitlement is relentlessly stoked? Could he have imagined the doomed pursuit of physical "perfection" that now haunts our children? We live in a society in which a common graduation gift of affluent parents to their teenage daughters is breast surgery—either implants or reductions. In seductive invitations to improve their bodies, our young people are being relentlessly pressed to damage them.

Freud himself may have had no talent for, or patience with, some contemporary psychopathologies, as he admittedly lacked the personal qualities to work with psychotic patients. Yet, as in the case of people suffering psychoses, I cannot imagine helping these newer patients without the concepts I have assimilated from Freud, without the appreciation of unconscious conflict itself, without his humbling and upsetting reminders that our rational faculties are far weaker than the synergy of our biological dispositions and our upbringing, and without his eventual conclusion that it is the loving relationship that cures. And neither can my colleagues of other orientations, whether they know it or not, as they continue to rediscover concepts, now arrayed in new nomenclature, that were originally postulated by Freud.

INTERPERSONAL CONFLICTS

Many of the other participants in the conversation this afternoon have mentioned the disturbing political developments of our time. Again, I cannot imagine trying to understand these without the Freudian concepts of projection and denial, the repetition compulsion, and the other psychic processes that Dr. Merlino has enumerated. How can we comprehend the passions of contemporary international antagonists without Freud's observations about the need to have an enemy—a dynamic he recognized in himself at both the personal level, in his comment about his ongoing need for both a supporter and a critic, and at the subcultural level in his identification as a "godless Jew" (Gay, 1987)? How else can we understand the sweet pleasure it gives us to see evil as coming from outside the self?

If we do not appreciate these processes in the twenty-first century, I think we are in deep trouble. How else can we comprehend the Islamic extremist's suicidal appetite for holy war? Or the fanatical determination of Taliban devotees to cover women in an effort not to feel desire? What sense could we make of the Christian extremists who try to avoid sexual ambiguity by vilifying homosexuality? Or of the terrifying genius of American political leaders who pander to our wishes to disown and project with concepts like "the enemy" and "the axis of evil"? Or even of the psychoanalytic fundamentalists who reject the foundational psychoanalytic stance of being willing not to know, whose paradigm wars distract us from reaching out beyond our professional communities and competitions to use our knowledge in the service of our fellow human beings?

The neuroscientist and psychoanalyst David Pincus recently summarized the enduring contributions of psychoanalysis as including the concepts of a dynamic unconscious, a valence to all mental life, a developmental viewpoint, the inevitability of conflict and defense, and the ubiquity of transferential processes (Pincus, 2006). If we lose these ultimately Freudian perspectives, our descendants may not see the twenty-first century through to the twenty-second.

NOTES

Fromm, E. (1947). *Man for himself: An inquiry into the psychology of ethics.* New York: Rinehart.

Gay, P. (1987). *A godless Jew: Freud, atheism, and the making of psychoanalysis.* New Haven: Yale University Press.

Kernberg, O. H. (1975). *Borderline conditions and pathological narcissism.* New York: Jason Aronson.

Kohut, H. (1971). The analysis of the self. New York: International Universities Press.

Pincus, D. (2006). Who is Freud and what does the new century behold? *Psychoanalytic Psychology* 23: 367–72.

Wolfenstein, M. (1951). *Fun morality: An analysis of recent American child-rearing literature.* In M. Mead and M. Wolfenstein (eds.), *Childhood in contemporary cultures* (pp. 168–78). Chicago: University of Chicago Press.

14

Freud in the Twenty-First Century

Eli Zaretsky

My title is meant to suggest a question: is Freud's thought solely of historical interest, or is it relevant to our lives today? Is Freud, in any meaningful
sense, still our contemporary, and if he is not, can he and should he become
one again? This talk is an attempt to answer this question. Let me begin it by
recalling why psychoanalysis once commanded such extraordinary attention
and why that changed.

To understand why psychoanalysis was once so compelling, it helps to
think of it as an uneasy synthesis of three different projects: a therapy or medical practice, a theory of culture, and an ethical current in everyday life. All
three of these projects ultimately arose from a common source: the global uprooting set in motion by mass consumption capitalism, along with such new
media as advertising and film. All three marked a profound change in Western thinking about the individual. Nevertheless, each project had a discrete
character and followed a distinct trajectory. Accordingly, I will take them up
in turn.

While history records many treatments for maladies of the soul, psychoanalysis was different in that it was based on an innovative psychological theory that viewed the human being as an arena of internal conflict. Individuals,
in Freud's conception, did not come to therapy simply to solve their problems. They also came to satisfy infantile wishes, wishes they simultaneously
struggled to suppress. According to Freudian theory, the drive to satisfy these
wishes, along with the drive to suppress them, was displaced onto a struggle
with the doctor or analyst. Only when that struggle subsided, and when the
patient accepted a certain defeat, could the real gain of the treatment reveal
itself, namely access to one's inner life and, perhaps, a certain restricted intimacy with the doctor. When viewed as a therapy, then, psychoanalysis was an

Freud with His Chow Chow, ca. 1920
Courtesy of Multiart.

ambitious project that far transcended medical aims. Even at the highpoint of its influence, it was clear that other treatments could relieve symptoms better than analysis. What psychoanalysis promised was different. It was the open-ended, noninstrumental, even "free" character of analysis that gave it its privileged place among therapeutic treatments.

The therapeutic project began as a solution to the riddle of the neurosis, a force that Freud called "inexpedient and running counter to the flow of life." To explain this riddle, Freud brought together British empiricism, which gave him the concept of the association of ideas, French medicine, which gave him the theory of transference, and German philosophy, which gave him the idea of the unconscious. He reconceptualized all three strands through the Darwinian vision of the human being as an organism driven by internal needs that it sought to satisfy in specific environmental niches. His solution to the riddle also reflected the influence of such sources as the Hebrew Bible and the Greek tragedians—works Freud traced to traumatic historical upheavals—and of everyday or "folk" understandings of psychology. Ultimately, Freud fused all of these currents into a powerful synthesis, neither wholly scientific nor wholly humanistic. This synthesis centered on the moral struggle of the human being, a struggle that arose in relation to the parents and that ended in the confrontation with death.

The therapeutic project converged with the second great project of psychoanalysis, its role as a cultural hermeneutic. Like an individual a culture can be viewed as having an unconscious. Just as in individual psychology, in which consciousness can be viewed as a sideshow with the main activity going on backstage, so religious rituals, political campaigns, novels, films or table manners can be viewed as screens, performances, expressions of defensive conflicts, efforts to keep order where no order exists. The original source for this idea of culture, an idea that worked its way into anthropology, literary criticism, cultural history and even artistic practice—think of the surrealists—was Freud's interpretation of dreams. Like dreams, cultural practices can be understood as palimpsests or archaeological sites: collections of traces, lay down in strata. Like dreams, cultures reveal slippages, fractures, inconsistencies, and distortions that require interpretation or decoding. Individuals respond to the slippages of culture in the same way that they remember their dreams, working over its unconscious content so that it is acceptable to the ego. Freudianism, by contrast, lent itself to a new way of reading culture, a hermeneutics of suspicion that directed attention to what was not openly said. Given that it developed amid an explosion of new media, such as film, advertisements, radio and TV, this unmasking function helps explain its widespread popularity.

At the same time, the Freudian theory of culture spoke to the need to come to somewhere that is the need to belong, which was so strong in that first age of global uprooting. But it spoke to the need to come from the species as a whole, and not from a particular nation or place. Drawing on comparative religion and mythology, archaeology and anthropology, on discoveries of ritual and totemism, non-Western family forms, mother goddesses, and stages of culture so "grey with age and shadowy" that they seemed to have "succumbed to an almost inexorable repression," Freud argued that every childhood relived the early history of the human species. In this view, half-remembered residues of traumatic cultural upheavals had established switch points along the path of individual development.[1] These switch points—orality, anality, bisexuality, the castration complex, the father complex, the Oedipus complex, latency, the superego—constitute a kind of grammar for culture, a grammar with analogues in mythology, religion and literature. Coinciding with the modernist orientation toward deep structures of subjectivity and interiority that could only be accessed from within, the Freudian focus on the interplay between the history of the individual and the history of culture was the second important reason for its compelling power.

The third strand comprising analysis, was the ethical project of self-reflection, which was especially important to young people and to the new middle-classes of the twentieth century. Seeking honesty and directness in personal life, as well as clarity and simplicity in such areas as architecture, design, and philosophical work, these new social strata assumed that a meaningful life necessitated self-reflection in depth. Sometimes the ethic of self-reflection was imbued with the passion of a calling, as when Floyd Dell called himself a "missionary" on the subject of psychoanalysis, or when Max Eastman said that he had become a kind of "amateur specialist." Underlying this ethic too was the new Freudian conception of the human subject. No longer the locus of universal reason, morality, and self-control as the Victorians pretended to believe, nor defined by a collectivity, as the socialists claimed, the twentieth century subject was a contingent, idiosyncratic mortal. Alienated from large-scale bureaucratic structures, he or she was typically intensely involved with a few love-objects or rivals leading to a rich, meaning-saturated, morally-inflected inner life. Analysis supplied the ethic for this life, an ethic based more on truth than on morality per se. In this regard, too, it marked an epochal step forward. Although sometimes attacked as amoral, psychoanalysis extended the pre-Freudian sense of personal responsibility to cover not only deliberate, conscious decisions but also unconscious actions. Encouraging the capacity to look at oneself objectively—"analytically"—and to enter empathically into other person's inner worlds, analysis discouraged moralism, while promoting the expansion of the moral capacity.

This third project—the psychoanalytic ethic, if one may speak that way—was never directly political, but neither could it be described as apolitical. To

begin with, Freud was typically read and discussed in the new milieus associated with artistic modernism, bohemia and Cultural Revolution, as well as
those, discussed below, of secular Jews, African-Americans and women.
Consider Lincoln Steffens' recollection of the first time—1910—that he was
introduced to the idea that "the minds of men were distorted by unconscious
suppressions." "There were no warmer, quieter, more intensely thoughtful
conversations at Mabel Dodge's [Greenwich Village salon]," Steffens wrote,
"than those on Freud and his implications." In Europe, especially central Europe but also England and even Russia, analysis was linked to socialist as
well as Zionist politics through polyclinics, sex-education and low-cost or
free analysis, as brought out in Elizabeth Danto's important recent book
Freud's Free Clinics. Even—perhaps especially—in periods of greatest alienation, analysis was never separated from political awareness. Thus Christopher Lasch recalled of the 1950s, "My generation invested personal relations
with an intensity they could hardly support . . . but our passionate interest in
each other's lives cannot . . . be described as a form of emotional retreat.
[Rather] we tried to re-create in the circle of our friends the intensity of a
common purpose, which could no longer be found in politics or the work-
place."

   The striking fact about these three projects—the therapeutic, the
hermeneutic, and the ethical—is that they were ever connected at all. Three
different projects, operating in different terrains, pursuing different aims, and
facing different obstacles: this labyrinth of different impulses nonetheless co-
hered. What held them together was the charisma of Freudianism and its conception of the human mind. Beginning in the 1970s, however, the three projects began to part ways. Since then, the therapeutic project has given way to
neuroscience, brain research, and psychopharmacology. The cultural
hermeneutic has been absorbed into popular culture in such forms as enter-
tainment and "cynical reason," as well as into cultural studies, feminist theory, "queer" theory, and the like. And the ethic of self-reflection has declined,
if not fallen away entirely. Let us now trace these divergent paths.

   Consider first the fate of analysis as a therapy. American analysts themselves sowed the seeds for the transformation of psychoanalytic practice into
neuroscience and pharmacology when they recuperated it into a medical
model from which it had originally diverged. The medical model diagnoses
illness on the basis of symptoms or tests and specifies treatment accordingly.
It therefore assumes a sharp distinction between the illness, for example cancer, and the patient, a person. Some psychological symptoms, such as compulsions, do conform to this model, but most do not. Most have to do with the
kind of inner division or conflict that I foregrounded earlier. Accordingly,
analysis should never have been reduced to depersonalized, objectified and,

in the case of mental health, often implicitly derogatory concepts. If analysis conformed to the medical model, how could it resist the quantitative, comparative outcome studies, behavioral techniques, and psychopharmacology favored by managed care? How could it resist legal tests of its scientific standing, as in the landmark case of Rafael Osheroff, the internist who was treated by analysts without success but who claimed to have been cured by drugs? How could it not defer to magnetic resonance imaging (MRI) and positron emission tomography (PET), which made it possible to observe the brain while mental operations were on-going? Today, most psychiatrists believe that the Freudian turn away from the study of the brain to the study of the unconscious mind was a huge, wasteful detour, and they have returned to the pre-Freudian brain science of Charcot, Kraepelin, and Bleuler.

If psychoanalysis has not fared well as a scientifically grounded medical practice, it might seem to have done better as a cultural hermeneutic. After the 1960s, the application of analytic concepts to cultural phenomena such as gender, nationality and sexual identity proliferated in almost every area of the humanities. Cultural politics replaced the Freudian cultural hermeneutic. But there was a big difference. During the Freudian epoch, the "unmasking" of culture reflected Freud's core belief that there was a tension between culture (or civilization) and the individual's "discontents." By contrast, the 1960s generation redefined the individual as always already cultural, cultural from the word go. The feminist movement of the 1970s supplied the paradigm. Against the analytic focus on intrapsychic reality, it called for an attack on the social and political structures of male oppression. "Individual explanations" were officially discouraged in "consciousness-raising" groups, while what had been forbidden or suspended within psychoanalysis—"acting out"—became privileged. The Oedipus complex was reinterpreted as a "power psychology." Penis envy was actually "power envy." There were good reasons for some of these changes, but they were one-sided, tending to transform psychoanalysis into a "recognition" or "other-directed" paradigm that was *un*psychological and *anti*psychological. In some cases, psychological concepts were restated in behavioral terms, as when the meaning of bisexuality shifted from inclinations *within* the individual to the question of which sex the individual slept with. In other cases, the destabilization of identity was taken as the harbinger of a more progressive society, as in much postmodern literature and thought. Thus, as one great slope of the psychoanalytic edifice disappeared into psychopharmacology and brain science, the other slid into identity politics.

Where did this leave the third great project associated with psychoanalysis, namely the ethical project of honesty, directness and self-knowledge? Simply put, a great deal of the energy once devoted to self-knowledge was given over to empowerment, sociability and group participation. In this regard, as in so many others, the fate of psychoanalysis was tied to a powerful social and cultural shift. Just as the *rise* of psychoanalysis was suffused by the fascination with private life that accompanied the advent of the great corporation, so the *decline* of psychoanalysis was associated with the birth of the polycentric, decentralized network society of today.

Let us return to our initial question: Is Freud, in any sense, our contemporary, and if he is not, can he and should he become one again? It is certainly no exaggeration to say that for most people Freud is no longer a living force in their lives. So the question we must ask now is whether that matters. After all, change is normal and every thinker becomes part of history, at least when they are lucky. As to the scientific standing of psychoanalysis, any empirically minded researcher expects, and even hopes, to become outmoded, the sooner the better. Why should we worry if the very complicated psychoanalytic picture of the mind, essentially the creation of one highly imaginative, dangerously charismatic, overly enthusiastic individual, has given way to a slow, steady collective effort to locate the mechanisms of memory, thought and emotion in the genes, amino acids, proteins and neurons of the brain? As for the project of cultural hermeneutics, our current understanding of the role that race, gender, sexual orientation, and ethnicity play in human life certainly corrects a political blindspot, or deliberate obfuscation, to which psychoanalysis sometimes lent itself.

Finally, what is there to say about the high value placed on self-exploration during the Freudian epoch? The long, pointless analyses, the hopeless pursuit of ever-receding insights, the turning of individuals into life-long patients, never quite submissive enough, never quite ready to leave their doctor: this all suggests that analytic self-knowledge was at the very least oversold. Why shouldn't empowerment, sociability and group identity replace self-knowledge, at least in part? In fact, the inward, self-reflective turn represented by psychoanalysis typically occurs only occasionally in life, for example, in adolescence, during traumatic interruptions such as object-loss, and perhaps in old age. The normal direction of the mind is outward, toward desired objects, with the aim of thwarting rivals and outmaneuvering obstacles. Whereas introspection did once define an epoch of social and cultural history—the Freudian epoch—there were contingent historical reasons for this, and it was bound to pass.

These are powerful arguments. I could believe them myself if it were not for a single reservation. The threefold analytic project had a critical dimension. Its conception of the human mind—its divisions, its switch-points in developmental traumata, its proneness to illusion—was linked to a notion of emancipation and even, at least until the 1950s, to the understanding that present-day society served the interests of the few rather than the many. Let me elaborate by clarifying what I mean by the term "critical."

Since the Enlightenment, and certainly since the democratic revolutions, a critical or "left" politics has refused to remain content with liberal ideals of freedom alone, seeking social equality as well. The liberal tradition argues that ever-expanding economic and technological progress combined with individual freedom and political democracy will lead to the realization of human wishes. The critical tradition stresses the inevitability of conflict and struggle. The liberal tradition is oriented to individual autonomy. The critical tradition shares with conservatives an awareness of the limits and connections that bind individuals to one another, especially through the family, through relations between the generations, and through our obligations as earth-sharing species. The liberal tradition takes ever-expanding choice as its ground. Ideally, the critical tradition is self-reflective. It is based on a sense of both our individual and collective past, and the way that past shapes whatever we do. In the twentieth century context, psychoanalysis supplied much of the impulse for critical self-reflection, as we can see if we consider each of its three projects.

The therapeutic assumption of internal psychical division portrayed the resistance to self-knowledge as powerful, loud and driven, while describing the desire for self-knowledge as light and soft, though persistent. In doing so, it at least identified a critical problem. The conception of therapy that followed, with its strongly confrontational aspects, was based on the Kantian idea of *Wissenschaft*, that is the idea that the unfolding of scientific knowledge should be accompanied by collective gains in self-knowledge rather than to the Baconian idea that the purpose of science was to satisfy unreflective human wishes. The aim of scientific advance was *Bildung*, an internal change in human beings, not technical advance per se. Even the analytic process, in this framework, though irreducibly committed to the relief of suffering, was a form of research, investigation and collective self-reflection. The more powerful our scientific advances becomes, as with the genome, cloning and neuroscience, the more important this self-reflective dimension of the scientific enterprise also becomes.

The analytic theory of culture also had a critical dimension. Mass society or, as it was then beginning to be called, consumer society equated individual autonomy with market choice. Psychoanalysis, in contrast, probed beneath the level of choice to its roots in unconscious instincts and wishes. Much of the interest in analysis came from those, such as Walter Lippmann or the Frankfurt School theorists, who rejected consumerism and mass culture as the moral basis of modern civilization. Thus, even as analysis encouraged psychological intimacy in the sphere of personal relations, it helped individuals to distance themselves from the sensate power of anonymous visual and aural images. This distancing, as I have suggested, was not apolitical. At a time when Western politics divided between authoritarians who rejected the Enlightenment, and proponents of instrumental rationality, "social planning" and Deweyan "intelligence," psychoanalysis defended "reason" in the classic sense of *Vernunft*. This defense, rooted in a stress on the psychological, familial and cultural prerequisites of democratic reform, had wide impact, especially during World War Two and its aftermath—for example, in the reconstruction of Germany or in the building of the postwar welfare states.

As to the ethic of self-reflection, every modern emancipatory movement has to decide how much weight to assign to the social determinants that inhibit freedom and how much to the responsibility that individuals have to gain freedom for themselves. The classical liberal tradition, which goes back to the seventeenth century, tended to overestimate the responsibility of the individual. The nineteenth century left, by contrast, overstated the social and economic obstacles to emancipation. Psychoanalysis helped restore the balance. Furthermore, I cannot indicate the ever-growing relevance of the ethic of directness and honesty better than by citing the words of Kurt Tucholsky, the editor of *Die Weltbühne*, the left-wing Weimar journal of the 1920s, who wrote that reforms "are of no use if a basic honesty (*Redlichkeit*) does not permeate the country."

Finally, the fact that three diverse projects had been fused into a unity was itself testimony to a critical orientation, because it brought out the ways in which all aspects of society were interconnected through a conception of the individual. Simply looking at a single individual, as Robert Musil noted in describing Moosbrugger, a carpenter on trial for cutting up a young girl in fin-de-siècle Vienna, was "like a loose end of a thread hanging out, and if one pulls at it, the whole tightly knit fabric of society begins to come undone."

The successors to psychoanalysis, by contrast, are not critical, at least not yet. Research into consciousness—as opposed to the unconscious—may eventually illuminate deeper, biological (self-preservative) motives for self-reflection than psychoanalysis knew, but this will only be a real gain if the interpretive and hermeneutic dimensions of psychotherapy are recuperated. Today, psychotherapy, like medicine and other service industries, has been reduced to the application of technical solutions to technical problems. Science, including the new neurosciences, produces new technologies all the time without anyone even imagining that these should be associated with a moral or ethical, much less emancipatory, change. As to the idea that culture is a screen or rationalization, it has become part of "cynical reason": since everyone knows how false our media-saturated world of celebrity, confession and life-stories is, what does it matter? Even the deep structure of duplicity that infuses what Vico called "the world of nations" is now often accepted as a norm, for example in electoral campaigns. And while today's focus on gender, race, sexual orientation and ethnic identity does have enormous critical content, that content remains undeveloped for two reasons. First, in rejecting "individual explanations" for a "power psychology," identity movements wound up affirming rather than questioning the Enlightenment premise that the sole goal of progress is to expand individual choices. And second, insofar as the content of these movements remains partial and self-interested, they lose what was so powerful in psychoanalysis, the aspiration toward universality, the conviction—to quote another great Austrian writer, Rudolf Carnap—that while "the fabric of life can never quite be comprehended . . . we must nonetheless always seek "the great lines which run through the whole." In sum, the dispersion of the analytic synthesis, its transformation into a series of three separate, unrelated projects, portended the destruction of its critical dimension.

We are now in a position to reformulate our original question, the question of whether Freud is of contemporary relevance. If we want to preserve the indisputable gains made by psychoanalysis, such as the theory of the unconscious, repression, and the internal object world, while incorporating the advances of our own day: feminism, gay liberation, and new theories of consciousness and recognition, we need to re-pose the question historically. I would suggest the following: How did a theory with a deep affinity with critical tendencies and movements in one period become absorbed into consumer culture, scientism and cynical reason in another?

In *Secrets of the Soul*, I suggested one approach to a solution by comparing the Freudian epoch and the Protestant reformation. In both cases, men and women were set adrift from what might be called "normal" forms of collective spiritual and psychological salvation. In both cases, the radical spiritual isolation of the individual was associated with a social transformation. The power of both Calvinism and psychoanalysis lay in the uncompromising way in which they spoke to trans-historical dilemmas of the human soul. Yet both played a catalytic role in precipitating historically specific changes. In the case of Calvinism, the change was the birth of capitalism; psychoanalysis, by contrast, served as the "Calvinism" of mass consumption, providing an *immanent* critique of the Protestant ethic at a time when that ethic had become dysfunctional, tempering the asceticism, compulsivity and hypocrisy that Max Weber associated with the Protestant ethic. The comparison between Calvinism and psychoanalysis provides a partial answer to the question of analytic ambiguity. During its early years, psychoanalysis was the cutting edge of a great cultural transformation: the rise of mass consumption with its effects on subjectivity, gender and family life. As such it helped facilitate the emergence of previously suppressed social groups. In its later years, it had become integrated into the Fordist Keynesian welfare state which the sixties generation subjected to attack.

Why did the new social movements of the twentieth century turn from supporting psychoanalysis to rejecting it? During the ascendancy of psychoanalysis in the first half of the twentieth century, it served as a corrective to over-socialized traditions of political radicalism, remedying *en bloc* understandings of the individual, according to which being a woman, an African-American, a Jew, or a worker, implied a particular psychology, stance or attitude. It thus helped emancipate particular oppressed groups during what I have called the Freudian century. During the second wave (which began in the 1960s), psychoanalysis came under attack for mystifying the preconditions of individuality, overvaluing those that were internal and ignoring or denigrating those that were collective and social.

The decline of psychoanalysis, or at least the loss of the privileged place it had occupied in Western culture began in the 1960s and was associated with profound changes in Western society. But this decline cannot be explained by external factors alone. Rather, we must look at the internal culture of psychoanalysis and ask how it interacted with the larger society's authoritarianism. The starting point for any such investigation must be the relation of analysts to Freud. Freud certainly had a bullying side although he was by no means the simple authoritarian his enemies portray. In addition, there was a way in which his conviction concerning his own genius, and his sense of always being at war with a hostile world, left his followers unprepared to carry on without him. Some awareness of this problem runs through the history of psychoanalysis: the conflicts with Adler and Jung, with Ferenczi and Rank, with Klein, with Adler, and the like.

Whatever Freud's conscious efforts, it does not seem that the psychoanalysts who survived him often lacked genuine independence and by this I mean, above all, independence from social and political pressures. I say this by consideration of what we might call the dark side of psychoanalysis. We can now see that this problem—the collaboration of analysts with legal but illegitimate authority—emerged with the rise of fascism and Nazism in the late 1920s and 1930s. As is now well known, until his death in 1939, Freud continued to communicate with the Berlin group purged as it was of Jews as if they represented psychoanalysis in Germany, apparently believing that psychoanalysis could survive in a racially-cleansed context. One should not expect heroic behavior. We should bear in mind Peter Gay's remark in his autobiography, *Growing up in Nazi Berlin*. "After spending years pondering this matter I remain convinced that our critics have never quite understood our dilemmas in the 1930s." Nonetheless, many groups have now gone back and rethought the experience of the 1930s and 1940s in light of contemporary standards of behavior, and we have every right to do the same for psycho-analysis.

The collaboration with authoritarianism reappears at many other points, but I will only mention one: U.S. ego psychology after World War II. Once again, to be fair, the 1950s were a conservative period, but analysts were on the extreme end of that conservatism. That was the period when analysis became, as one analyst boasted, "the brand that . . . dominates the market," or, in Alfred Kazin's words, a "big business and a very smooth one."[2] Nevertheless, psychoanalysis was often a community in bad faith, boasting successes and ignoring failures, distorting classroom presentations, and denying itself the means for self-correction. When I was doing research for my history of psychoanalysis in the 1990s, I asked everyone I met who had been in analysis how they felt about their experience: overall, most were extremely negative, at least about their "first" analysis. To this day, no one really knows how many "failures," second and third analyses, and lives tragically distorted, American analysts produced.

These reflections return us to our original question: the contemporaneity of psychoanalysis. Is Freud's thought essentially of historical interest, or is it relevant to our lives today? The answer, I believe we can now see, is that this is a false choice. History plays a role for society analogous to the role that memory plays for the individual. A people who does not know its history will be disoriented, much like an individual who does not know his or her history. To understand psychoanalysis historically, then, is the necessary prerequisite to making it our contemporary.

Let me end with a final observation. Freud's image—his imago, to use an analytic term—did not succumb to the slow processes of deidealization and mourning that normally characterizes the passing on of a major figure and that we associate with historical understanding. Rather, much of Freud's true character, and much of the actual contribution of psychoanalysis, was distorted through a series of explosive, demagogic and profoundly misleading attacks. Paradoxically, Freud became a historical figure to those who respected and even revered him, while to his enemies he remains a vital, intensely cathected contemporary. This suggests that the question of whether Freud is still our contemporary has not been resolved.

NOTES

1. Freud, *SE*, 21, p. 226.
2. Alfred Kazin, "The Freudian Revolution Analyzed," *New York Times Magazine*, May 6, 1956, p. 22.

Freud's Place in Our Minds

The Significance of Sigmund Freud in the Twenty-First Century

Sheila Hafter Gray*

I hope that at the conclusion of this essay you will be able to discern the influence of Freud's experience and education on his approach to the care of patients and to clinical research, and to decide for yourselves if Freud is, or ought to be, a model for contemporary clinical scientists.

In the twenty-first century we value diversity, and I want to remind us that Freud was inherently an outsider. He was a Jew among Catholics in a remnant of the Holy Roman Empire, for that is what Austria was at that time. He had his place there because the Habsburg emperor protected minorities and this, to an important extent, mitigated against the effects of indigenous anti-Semitism. This allowed him to compete for—and to gain—a place in the university, which afforded him a good education, but while he was in that environment, he was on its periphery.

He had fellowship education in France, which was outside the Viennese university establishment. That taught him a different approach to the practice of medicine. In France, clinical observation was always privileged over theory or laboratory findings, as it was at the Harvard Medical School in the United States, whereas the Germans preferred scientific to clinical truth, an approach well exemplified here by the Johns Hopkins University (Beecher and Altschule, 1977). So Freud returned from France knowing how to focus on patients. To quote one of my own professors, "Listen to the patient. She, or he, will tell you the diagnosis." And that, precisely, is what Freud did.

* Disclaimer: The opinions or assertions contained in this presentation are the private views of the author and are not to be construed as official or as reflecting the views or policies of the U.S. Department of Defense or any of its associated institutions.

His outsider status was his strength. Because he had different points of view, he could have empathy for the other. That allowed him to listen attentively to what were then considered the irrational ravings of hysterical housewives. He could feel his way into their emotional life, and, therefore, he could create innovations in the clinical care of these individuals. Also, he was able to integrate a variety of perspectives from art, archaeology, medicine, surgery, and literature, with all of which he was familiar, and to integrate them into a comprehensive theory—actually the first complete bio-psycho-social model that we know—a model that explains in one theory the body and the mind, the individual, and society, of each unique person.

Where would we locate Freud in today's healthcare practice?

Some of you know about evidence-based medicine. Very briefly David Sackett (1996) who invented it, calls it the "the conscientious, explicit and judicious use of current best evidence in making decisions about the care of individual patients." It is research based, but the evidence from clinical research takes precedence over theoretical concepts and basic research that may use animal models rather than individual human beings.

If you look back at Freud's work, he practised evidence-based medicine as we understand it correctly today. He used the research techniques of his generation, which were case studies and clinical-pathological correlations. If you look at his papers, they are in form the same as surgical papers or medical papers of that time. This is the way people wrote about their patients. He applied the relevant scientific findings from a variety of disciplines to improve clinical practice. I will mention only one: The personal equation was something that has bothered astronomers for generations. They knew that no two people had the same reaction time. If one tries to observe a star and press a button when a phenomenon is first seen, there is always a variation among individuals, a variation that cannot be eliminated by training (Boring, 1957). Astronomers finally decided that each person would get his own personal equation that could be used to correct his observations. And that is, if you think about it, very similar to the origin of our training analysis. When we learn what we contribute to the process, we can approach the patient and discern what is the patient's contribution and what is our own contribution to the interaction, and we also learn about the patient through a study of his or her effect on us.

Again, Freud was a person who privileged the clinical over the laboratory, and particularly in his case, developmental neurohistology.

He also practiced something about which you may know less—narrative-based medicine. This is more a feature of primary care medicine than of psychiatry (Greenhalgh, 2002). In that specialty they believe that medicine is best taught and remembered as stories about patients. Also, intuition is an essential skill for clinical practice and to generate scientific hypotheses. But, they point out, this requires systematic critical reflection about one's intuitive judgements *via* creative writing, dialogue with colleagues, etc. In Britain they have Balint groups that are essentially a kind of a support group, helping physicians deal with their feelings about patients, using those feelings to generate an understanding of what is going on in the patient, etc. And here again you can see the role of personal analysis and self analysis in the practice of ordinary day to day medicine.

What Freud would not have practiced is evidence-based treatment. That, I think, is the focus of Professor Zaretsky's critique. Evidence-based—or empirically supported—treatment involves randomized control trials, manual-driven uniform interventions, and measured outcomes (Kazdin, 2006). It focuses on group statistics and discounts the individual case. It is true that no one has been able to study psychoanalysis in this way, but some venturesome colleagues cheerfully construct psychotherapy manuals and run clinical trials (Clarkin, Kernberg, and Yeomans, 1999; Milrod et al., 2007). For the past 15 years empirically supported treatment has been a great driving force, but now people are reconsidering. They are returning to investigation of *TAU* (treatment as usual), in which one forges a specific treatment for each patient. This is essentially a craft. It is not science; it is something that clinician and patient co-construct to meet the latter's individual needs. It was used as the control or active placebo for trials of manual-based therapy. They found that it worked much better than the experimental treatment. Clinicians are actually able now to study these treatments, including psychoanalysis, using new investigative techniques. I shall mention just the psychotherapy process Q-sort and new statistical tools that analyse changes in individuals rather than in groups. Those are patient-centred researches that are clinically relevant (Ablon et al., 2006).

I shall mention one further thing that I wish were still true but that I fear is not. I wish we could write in a way that facilitates people understanding what we say. I will remind you that Freud was awarded the Goethe Prize. He was honored for the literary quality of his scientific writings because that supported a deep understanding of patients and of his theory. In Germany today they award a Freud Prize for the best written scientific paper in German language. The winner can come from any science—it is the language that counts. This is a contemporary recognition that beautiful prose helps the reader grasp and remember the subject matter of any discipline.

NOTES

Ablon, J. Stuart, Raymond A. Levy, and Tai Katzenstein. Beyond brand names of psychotherapy: Identifying empirically supported change processes. *Psychotherapy: Theory, Research, Practice* 43 (2006): 216–31.

Beecher, Henry K. and Mark D. Altschule. *Medicine at Harvard: The First 300 Years.* Hanover NH: The University Press of New England, 1997.

Boring, Edwin G. *A History of Experimental Psychology*, 2nd ed. New York: Appleton-Century Crofts, 1957.

Clarkin, John F., Otto F. Kernberg, and Frank E. Yeomans. *Transference-Focused Psychotherapy for Borderline Personality Disorder Patients.* New York: Guilford Press, 1999.

Greenhalgh, Tricia. Intuition and evidence—uneasy bedfellows? *British Journal of General Practice* 52 (2002): 395–400.

Kazdin, Alan E. Arbitrary metrics: Implications for identifying evidence-based treatments. *American Psychologist* 61 (2006): 42–49.

Milrod, Barbara, Andrew C. Leon, Fredric Busch, Marie Rudden, Michael Schwalberg, John Clarkin, Andrew Aronson, Meriamne Singer, Wendy Turchin, E. Toby Klass, Elizabeth Graf, Jed J. Teres, and M. Katherine Shear. A randomized controlled clinical trial of psychoanalytic psychotherapy for panic disorder. *American Journal of Psychiatry* 164 (2007): 265–72.

Sackett, David L., William M. C. Rosenberg, J. A. Muir Gray, R. Brian Haynes, and W. Scott Richardson. Evidence based medicine: What it is and what it isn't. (Editorial). *British Medical Journal* 312 (1996): 71–72.

Freud into the Ages

Harold Blum

Regarding Freud's status in the twenty-first century, of all things, the hardest to predict is the future. I think that given Freud's contributions to the understanding of human nature, it is quite likely that Freud's theories, his ideas, and his discoveries about human nature will persist, until the human genome changes. I have come to this conclusion for the following reasons: Freud applied psychoanalytic thought to medicine, psychology, and the humanities. He also validated his formulations by integrating material from a variety of sources. Freud used the Oedipus complex in references to Greek myths, to Shakespeare, and to Goethe for particular purposes. He wanted to demonstrate that the ideas that he had found listening to his patients and in his own self-analysis could be found in the art and literature of the past and across different cultures. The most important aspect of the Oedipus complex from that point of view is that Freud discovered in Sophocles' drama "Oedipus Rex" the same conflicts that he found in his patients and in himself. When he realized that Hamlet, across the centuries, represented some of the same conflicts to be found in Sophocles, he was able to unify past and present, normal and pathological phenomena. He could verify and validate his concepts and show that they didn't just apply to people in Vienna, not just to Jews or Christians but to all peoples and through all times. Sometimes excoriated as a Jewish pervert, Freud asserted that his discovery about the unconscious applied to people of all races.

We have actually seen across the twentieth century, Freud-bashing and today recurrent Freud-bashing, sometimes of a fanatic nature. The fact is that we have had periods of appreciation of psychoanalysis, of idealization of psychoanalysis, and then periods of devaluation and derision. These attitudes have fluctuated. Freud was accused of being a phrenologist, a palmist, a charlatan, and so on, at the same time that he was gathering students, disciples, and adherents. This ambivalent reaction went on and on, and we have to ask ourselves why the challenges now seem greater. Eli Zaretsky brought up some important points—I want to add another point: We live in an age of a plethora of psychoanalytic theories, a time of psychoanalytic pluralism. Freud probably, in his own reflective thinking, might infer today "Well, that's the anticipated course of development in a discipline." There are always new pathways, new developments; it is not to be expected that later generations would see the things the same way as he did. Had he lived, he would doubtless have changed his own views as his thought evolved and new knowledge became available. Some of his ideas, however, remain unchanged and are at the core of the way we understand patients today. For example, the concept of transference was first formulated in relation to the case of patient Anna O. in the early 1880s. She was actually Breuer's patient, and you may recall that in 1895 Breuer and Freud published the book *Studies on Hysteria*. Freud was not listening to that patient, Breuer was. Breuer, who was actually a doctor of internal medicine, was like a fish out of water in attempting the hypnotherapy on his own. The "talking cure" was developed with the collaboration of this very extraordinary patient. It was her name for the treatment. (Anna O. was the designated name in English because the patient had lost the capacity to speak in German.) Freud can be thought of as in the role of a supervisor at some distance from the case treated by Breuer. He discovered what he was beginning to see in himself and other patients—the phenomenon of transference and counter-transference between doctor and patient.

Over time, psychoanalysis has undergone major modifications and has been combined with other therapeutic modalities, for example, psychopharmacology. One of the most important legacies of psychoanalysis is its popular application for vast members of the population. Psychoanalysis gave rise to dynamic psychotherapy, also called psychoanalytic psychotherapy or insight psychotherapy. Freud's discoveries—the importance of transference, the doctor patient relationship, the importance of defenses, the understanding of unconscious conflict and fantasy, insight into the nature of the therapeutic process and outcome—all are derived from psychoanalytic theory and principles.

Freud has become part of our language—namely, the Oedipus complex, libido, defenses, projection, denial, and repression. Despite the numerous critiques of Freud, he remains so much a part of our culture, of the intellectual climate of our time and the past century, that these terms and formulations are taken for granted without Freud's being acknowledged. Terms like denial and repression are used without reference to their psychoanalytic source. Plays are analyzed by the audience and by the drama critics. They analyze conflicts, characters, and so forth without really bringing up the fact that drama criticism was completely different before Freud and after Freud. Human conflict, the analysis of character, and motive was very different before Freud. You only have to read Samuel Taylor Coleridge's descriptions and criticisms of Shakespeare compared to contemporary critics of Shakespeare. Freud found also in the great poets further inspiration and acknowledgement of his ideas. Recently we had the case of a person who confessed supposedly to having killed a girl, apparently his fantasy. We know that Freud wrote a paper on unconscious guilt that persists from childhood.

I think Zaretsky is correct in that patients come because they want their wishes to be satisfied, but I would add that the patient is not aware of these unconscious wishes. They come to treatment because they are experiencing symptoms. They come because they are anxious and depressed and distressed, and behind these emotions are forbidden wishes. Behind the defenses and what you call the secondary revision, the facade of their presenting complaints, are infantile wishes along with their infantile defenses and prohibitions. Now I also want to bring up the fact that even the way we understand symbolism is taken for granted. If someone talks about a banana or a rocket or a sword as a phallic symbol, it's known today, it's nothing new. But of course before Freud it was not known—if one looks at the symbol of a sword as a phallus and a cave or cavity as representing the female genitals, we understand that almost without thinking about it. But when Edgar Allen Poe wrote "The Pit and the Pendulum," that was not understood in terms of sexual relations—the pit representing the female organ and the pendulum symbolizing the male sexual organ, and the swinging back and forth representing copulation. All of this, which is now part of the way we think, was not really understood at all pre-Freud. I want to say something further about the way in which Freud was a great unifier. He took the literature—Shakespeare, Sophocles, Goethe, and others—he looked at art, he analyzed Leonardo, gave us the first psychobiography, all interrelated with the structure of dreams and memories and fantasy. Freud gave us the first interpretations of dreams; before Freud, dreams were either considered divine messages from upon high or messages from the devil and divinations. Sorcerers and oracles were the ones to whom people turned for understanding dreams, or they were given symbolic interpretations far removed from the understanding that Freud offered. He showed how dreams have basically the same structure as symptoms, as aspects of character, play, and drama. He linked the child and the adult and showed that the child is very much alive in the adult. This unification of symptoms, dreams, character, transference, the child in the adult, were all things that were not understood before Freud. It is very important to understand, too, that the way we think in the century of the child did not occur before Freud and was not really understood in the same way. We know today how important child rearing is, how important child development is for the personality of the adult. This was not something that was understood pre-Freud in the same way at all. Nor was the understanding of regression. We know today that people act like infants; adults can act like children in a few moments—you just have to go to a football game to see this. Ordinary people can be observed treating each other violently. This kind of mob response where an adult mind becomes childlike is in many respects what we call regression. There can also be progression very quickly in the other direction, growing up again very quickly in a reversal of regression. Psychological regression is not paralleled in organic medicine. Our bone structure doesn't change as we become adults. This regression-progression flow, the understanding of regression to childhood continues into adult life. I expect Freud will persist into the indefinite future as part of intellectual history and scientific development.

We live in a time of great violence, and perhaps we always have had great violence. We live in a time of tremendous traumatization. We had hope for rational solutions to international conflicts after World War II and the formation of the United Nations. We longed for stability without regressions into the most primitive reactions as though going back to cave men times. Freud's important formulations of psychic trauma are relevant to the understanding and treatment of victims of terror and violence. There can be psychic trauma with or without physical trauma. People can be severely traumatized, mentally and physically, as they were during World War II, in concentration camps and in the holocaust, and as they are today in Iraq and in many other parts of the world. What did Freud discover about trauma? He discovered the importance of obligatory repetition of a tendency and a need to repeat the trauma, of defenses against repeating the trauma. Trauma is relived in the form of nightmares, flashbacks, haunting memories, and so forth. Traumatized persons become hypervigilant and lose basic trust. They are inwardly afraid and are readily alarmed. Someone who has been traumatized may overreact to the sound of a siren or of a fire engine. Psycho-physiological reactions are common in severely traumatized persons. Freud was the first one to really describe psychic trauma in depth. (Freud began as a neurologist and wrote a very important book about aphasia.) Although we have subsequently added to trauma theory, the importance of psychic trauma remains, and the analytic method of treating it remains. Recently neuroscience has made very important contributions to the psychobiology of trauma. Sometimes regarded as a competitor of psychoanalysis, it also validates and is synergistic with psychoanalysis. Neuroscience has demonstrated that certain changes, for example in the hippocampus and amygdala, occur with traumatization. Freud wrote that severe trauma may permanently affect the energic qualities of the mental processes. He was aware of the effect of the mind on the brain and of the brain on the mind. Freud knew that in dreaming sleep, the voluntary muscular system is paralyzed; otherwise people would act out their dreams. The relationship with neuroscience is very complicated, and there is reason to hope in the century of the brain, the new twenty-first century, that psychoanalysis and neuroscience will stimulate and enrich each other. Although evolving along different pathways, the two disciplines will intertwine as they confront issues of mutual concern.

Thousands of years ago the Delphic Oracle was regularly consulted. People came with their problems and ills expecting some kind of divine cure. At least the oracle would have an omniscient understanding and would offer help to the sufferer. Disturbed persons brought their dreams; they would have sleep therapy. The oracle would interpret the dream and the healed patient would offer votive tablets on which they would describe their cures. Like people hanging up their crutches in church, the ancients testified to how much they had been helped by this method. It was a forerunner of dream interpretation, much like Joseph's interpretation of the dreams in the Bible. The Delphic Oracle had an adage which I think still is important even though it is not respected or valued in much of the world. Her adage and her model was "know thyself," and I think in many ways that maxim still remains very valuable for all of us, even to the present day and beyond.

NOTES

Freud, S. (1891). Zur Auffassung der Aphasien, Vienna. Trans.: On Aphasia, London and New York, 1953.

Freud's Voice

Nancy McWilliams

I want to argue that Freud's significance for this new century can be thorough-going—and positive—only if we as a community can preserve his unique voice. I am using the term "voice" both literally and as a metaphor for something much more elusive and ephemeral; namely, a sensibility or ethos. This sensibility goes even beyond Auden's "climate of opinion" to something broader, a profoundly paradigm-shifting attitude toward life and human experience.

Think with me about the voice for a minute. My friends may know two things about me which—I nod to Freud here—are doubtless complexly re-lated. I am passionately interested in individuality and individual differences (including Freud's idiosyncratic personality) and I am an amateur singer. Singers talk a lot about voices, about what songs are good "in your voice," about whether the voice is full or tight, resonant or thin, on pitch or off, able to convey emotion, able to capture nuance, able to move an audience. In or-dinary parlance, we make frequent observations about people's voices: whether they are warm and rich or shrill and grating, whether they welcome us in or keep us out, whether they sound ragged or gravelly or anxious or in-sincere or smarmy or whiny.

Informally and unselfconsciously, we all note vocal differences. The voice is a kind of signature. Except for identical twins, no two people seem to have identical voices. (And in the case of identical twins, perhaps I am not alone in finding vocal identicality somehow more viscerally disturbing than visual identicality.) We recognize voices quickly, and sometimes, without quite knowing how we do it, we can imitate another's voice. We have recently learned that infants know their mother's voice even before they emerge from her body. Her voice is their first object, the first evidence of their relationship with a separate subjectivity.

In psychosis, people hear voices. In fact, we all hear voices. Patients, during psychotherapy and afterward, hear their therapist's voice alongside other inner voices. Their internal choir gets a new singer, one whose song may be sweeter or more comforting or braver than those who came before. Voices live on in our heads long after the speaker has left us.

We can't describe voices very well; we must settle for being impressionistic. Still, I am going to try to describe the kind of voice Freud had. I heard Freud's actual voice only once, in a recording Theodor Reik had made toward the end of his mentor's life. At that time, Freud's voice was painfully compromised by throat cancer and the prosthesis that it required, and it sounded weak and weary. His accent was oddly jarring to me, given that everything I had read in his voice had been translated into English; English was the language he spoke in my head. What came through was warm, authoritative, passionate, and wise, but in what I am about to say, I am depending less on these impressions than on those of his patients and colleagues, and on the gestalt that comes through in his writing.

Freud's patients (e.g., Kardiner, Doolittle, Blanton) generally describe him as warm and compassionate, as he sounded to me. He was also intensely curious. As Judith Kaplan noted, he enjoyed raising questions even more than he enjoyed answering them. He loved to play with ideas; he retained the child's eager curiosity about how things work, about how diverse phenomena may interconnect. Who else could have thrown together psychopathological symptoms, psychotic states, nocturnal dreaming, slips of the tongue, and jokes, and assumed that they are all related? Only in a post-Freudian world are such connections in any way self-evident.

Freud was both speculative and opinionated, tentative and authoritative. I suspect that this combination is intimately related to the elusive phenomenon of charisma, and to the curious polarization that still arises when Freud's name is invoked. When he spoke dogmatically, Freud would move instantly from one or a few instances to a universal. He would make specific discoveries with his female patients and then expound upon female psychology as a general topic. He would notice a dynamic in himself and insist that it could be found in anyone.

This universalizing was both wonderful and problematic. For example, a careful study of his own history suggests that Freud had a deeply bisexual nature. His sexual experiences, so far as we know, were with women, but if we take seriously Helen Fisher's findings that we all have at least three love systems—a sexual system, a romantic system, and an attachment system—it is pretty clear that Freud's romantic and attachment systems were organized around male objects. All of his really passionate relationships, his intoxicating idealizations and his agonizing estrangements, involved men. Given this psychology, Fleiss's notion of our inherent bisexuality must have resonated powerfully in Freud. When he recognized the truth of an assertion for himself, he tended to make the leap that it was true for everyone; hence, his conviction that a core analytic task for every man entails accepting his homosexual strivings. Speaking clinically, I have worked with some men for whom this was a central issue and with some in whom it was a marginal or perhaps even absent question.

On the other hand, generalizing in this way opened the door to normalizing homosexuality and to encouraging putatively heterosexual individuals to consider whether their psychology had a homoerotic dimension. It expanded our intrapsychic possibilities in a non-shaming, accepting way. Freud's universalizing from his own dynamics and from those of his patients tended to put off many colleagues in his own time and has offended many enduring critics in ours. But at the same time, this deep conviction that if he could find it in himself, it must be true for all human beings, may have been his most humane legacy. In an era of arrogance about the superiority of civilized people over "savages," Freud found common ground with the savages, and with human beings of all eras and cultures. The inclusiveness of his voice has been precious.

Freud's voice was also disciplined and absorbent; before Bion and Winnicott, he intuitively knew something about holding and containing. As Kirsner has recently argued, he was a stoic person, who did not shrink before harsh realities and talked in terms of necessary compromises. No stranger to grief, he was keenly aware of limits and resigned to what is possible. He was sardonic, he loved a good joke, and his humor was not without sadism. Yet he was in critical ways assiduously respectful. When other physicians were dismissing women with hysterical symptoms as malingerers, Freud took them seriously. Irrespective of my disagreements with many of Freud's generalizations about women, as a woman and a feminist I have been enduringly appreciative of that respectful, egalitarian tone.

Freud's voice was also poetic. He could do the words *and* the music. Dr. Hafter-Gray has mentioned his Goethe prize for literature; even in translation, he is one of the preeminent stylists of the last century. He was deftly rhetorical. Unlike colleagues of similar intelligence and originality—Pierre Janet, for example, who was probably closer to right than Freud was in their disagreement about dissociation versus repression—Freud was a skilled propagandist for his ideas and thus captured the public imagination. In his effective use of parable to tell subtle and sometimes unpalatable truths, he was second only to Jesus.

Notwithstanding his stoicism and his thoroughgoing logical positivism, this determined rationalist was also a romantic and sometimes spoke in a romantic voice. Theodor Reik tells of how he went to Freud with a question about a major life decision. Freud responded that he believed that for all relatively unimportant choices in life, one should examine the alternatives with scrupulous rationality, thinking through the pros and cons, weighing the options. For significant life decisions, however, such as what profession to pursue or what person to marry, one had to follow one's heart and leave the choice to one's deeper nature.

Finally, Freud's voice was embracing. He was not simply open to, and educated in, a wide range of disciplines (anthropology, archeology, literature, languages, history, mythology, evolutionary theory, physics), he was also sensitive to the coexistence of apparent opposites, the ubiquity of ambiguity, the power of paradox. How different this voice is from that of the contemporary—dare I say brainwashed—American therapist-in-training who asks (as two talented, certifiably well educated, and intelligent graduate students asked me this past year), "What is this term you use: ambivalence?" How different from the contemporary colleague who insists, whenever the discussion turns to some complex manifestation of human suffering, "There's a manual for that." I could tolerate losing many of Freud's specific ideas and opinions if I could count on our keeping alive his voice, his sensibility.

Let me end with a quote from Freud himself: "The voice of the intellect is a soft one but it does not rest until it has gained a hearing." I hope he was right.

A Day of Reflection on Freud's Significance in the Twenty-First Century

Miriam Pierce

The early beginnings of social work and its interface with psychoanalytic thought and practice are relevant to Freud's significance in this century. Travel back with me to the turn of the twentieth century; the beginning of Freud's clinical observations and discoveries on the workings of the mind. He wanted to establish psychoanalysis as a method of treatment and as a new science of the mind. He wrote about the unconscious as it influenced the "everyday life" of the individual and as a form of treatment that could alleviate suffering from neurotic symptoms. Social work in the United States was in its beginnings, and it concerned itself with the needs and suffering of the poor; "their misery of every day life" and its impact on children and families. Immigrants were flooding the cities, which were unprepared to provide basic services. Child labor laws had not yet been enacted. Working conditions, all too often in sweatshops, were terrible. The social security system did not come into existence until the 1930s. It was left to volunteer agencies and religious organizations to provide services. Social work as a profession was the response to these most difficult environmental stressors.

Mary E. Richmond, an early social work clinician, under the auspices of the Russell Sage Foundation, published *Social Diagnosis* in 1917, a text written to provide caseworkers with a tool for assessing and diagnosing these multidetermined problems. Social workers, in the main, were actively engaged in working with children, delinquents, the courts, medical facilities and families in crisis. To quote from her text:

> When a human being, whatever his economic status, develops some marked form of social difficulty and social need, what do we have to know about him and about his difficulty before we can arrive at a way of meeting his need. The

problem may be one of childhood or old age, of sickness, of exploitation, of wasted opportunity, but, insofar as it concerns some one individual in his social relationships, it is not alien to social work as here understood. (Richmond, 1917, p. 26)

Therefore, when the doctor or judge perceives social workers as an adjunct to his clinic or court, he may have but a dim idea of the distinctive contribution of authenticated and interpreted social fact that they should bring to his professional work. In this case, he tends to fit them into the traditions of his own calling and to ignore the characteristics of theirs" (Richmond, 1917, p. 36). She was emphasizing the need for mutual respect and collaboration between the disciplines.

Social work in the 1920s was looking for assistance in understanding clients in order to enhance their functioning; it recognized that simply manipulating the systems and giving advice was insufficient. Psychoanalysis was being noticed by social workers and other professions. Sigmund Freud lectured at Clark University in Worcester, Massachusetts, in 1909. He talked about the unconscious, self-destructive behaviors, anxieties, defenses, transferences. Social workers related to Freud's philosophy that the poor man or woman had as much right to help for mental problems as did any other in the community and that psychotherapy should be offered to enhance functioning. Psychoanalysis was a compassionate and empathic therapeutic therapy; this certainly was a basic tenet in social work practice. Caseworkers then adopted a psychosocial diagnosis that included psychological functioning in their assessment for working with clients. Some social workers undertook their own psychoanalysis, and by the 1930s clinical social workers were applying psychoanalytic psychodynamic thinking in their work. Social work continued, as a profession, however, to take into account both the external as well as the internal world.

As social work focused on children and families, it is not surprising that family therapy, as a new model of treatment, evolved from work in the then-existing social agencies. Nathan Ackerman, a psychoanalyst working at a family agency, was the founder of a psychodynamic family therapy. However, we could date back the first family treatment to Freud's case Little Hans. This is the case of a four-year-old child suffering from a phobia of horses that, in 1909 Vienna, kept him quite restricted as he was afraid to leave his home. He had been a healthy, quite exuberant little boy before the phobia took hold. He then became sad and worried, with a loss of energy that worried his parents. His parents were adherents of Freud and attended meetings that Freud would hold for interested professionals and parents. Hans's father approached Freud with his little boy's worries and symptoms to ask his advice and guidance. Little Hans was subsequently written up as one of Freud's five famous cases.

While Freud did not treat Little Hans directly, he was interested in demonstrating the infantile neurosis in *status nacendi*. He decided he would consult with the father to ask for reports of the child's worries. Freud would assist the father in the interpretation of these fears. Little Hans saw Freud for only one visit, and Freud was impressed with this child's curiosity and mind. Little Hans was primarily helped by the collaborative work between Freud and his father. One might well say, as Martin Silverman (1980) wrote, that this was, indeed, the first family therapy case. The good result that was obtained could be understood as not only psychoanalytic understanding of the phobia but the feeling of safety that the father was able to provide his son as Hans revealed fears of his father's anger and aggression as well as his own angry wishes toward his father. Understanding the developmental phases of childhood, the anxieties that children struggle with, and the need to master these childhood anxieties was instrumental in enabling Freud to support this father and, in turn, enabling this father to provide the support his son needed from him.

While Freud was primarily interested in phallic oedipal conflicts when he wrote the Little Hans case, there was much evidence that a history of earlier trauma had impacted Little Hans. Baby-watching as a method of research had not yet been incorporated into psychoanalytic theory. Anna Freud, a child analyst, was most concerned with developmental issues in childhood. When the Freuds escaped the Nazis and relocated in Hampstead, London, she became involved with the children in the Hampstead War Nursery. She observed that separation from parents proved, at times, to be more traumatic for the children when they were relocated to the safety of the countryside. Later, at the Anna Freud Center in London, she and her colleagues designed a developmental profile of early childhood as an instrument to assess children. This instrument is still widely used today.

Freudian theory was expanded and modified to include the studies of "baby watchers" who would observe babies in their natural environment in order to follow patterns of infant behavior. In the 1950s Rene Spitz studied and wrote on the first year of life, giving psychoanalytic theory an expanded view of development. Margaret Mahler, trained as a pediatrician and psychoanalyst, conducted research in early childhood development and with her colleagues, Pine and Bergman, published a book on the psychological birth of the human infant (Mahler et al, 1978).

In the 1970s, Berry Brazelton, a noted pediatrician and child psychoanalyst, studied newborns and developed a competency scale as both a medical tool and a tool that could be used as a way to help parents understand their newborn's capacities and their baby's cues. Contemporary baby-watching and infant-parent psychotherapy was inspired by Selma Fraiberg's clinical work. She was first trained as a social worker before she undertook a medical degree. The model of psychoanalytically oriented infant-parent psychotherapy as an intervention was originally proposed in the article, "Ghosts in the Nursery," by Fraiberg, Adelson, and Shapiro (1975). This seminal paper continues to be cited as the inspiration for the clinical work currently being done in infant observation and research.

In recent years there has been a burgeoning of research in infant development. Attachment theory has been studied by psychoanalysts interested in understanding the potential for its application to clinical practice and research. Infant researchers Beebe, Stern, and Fonagy, to name just a few, have integrated psychoanalytic concepts with the findings of attachment theory. Environmental and socioeconomic concerns, as they impact on the infant's physical and psychological development, have been integrated into the thinking of infant researchers. Neuroscience has illuminated the development of the infant's brain and directs our attention to the significance of the infant-mother interaction for right-side brain development in the first three months of life. As the brain continues to develop in subsequent months, the dyadic relationship, as a co-constructed endeavor, is crucial for the infant's developing mind. Ainsworth's "Strange Situation," based on attachment theory, is currently being applied to many different situations in the research of infant-parent relationships and child development.

This is where we are at the turn of the twenty-first century: Reflecting on the collaboration between the disciplines as they inform and respect each other's work. It brings to mind the major contribution made by the collaborative work of Anna Freud, Goldstein, and Solnit when they wrote the books *Beyond the Best Interests of the Child, Before the Best Interests of the Child,* and *In the Best Interests of the Child.* This was an effort to influence the courts in decisions regarding the disposition of the care of children in divorce, adoption and foster care. This work was done under the auspices of the Yale Child Study Center, which continues to do innovative work with children and families. The staff works within the community and they are psychoanalysts. They have learned that understanding the community is essential to working effectively when providing service. Parent infant programs have also influenced policy making on a federal level. "The Babies Can't Wait Law" that was passed in the 1990s is a law that promotes permanency for the under-one-year-old baby in foster care.

Innovative work has been undertaken by both the New York Freudian Society and the Institute for Psychoanalytic Research and Training in New York. They now have a collaborative program, The Anni Bergman Parent-Infant Training Program. I think it is of interest to mention, given that this conference is being held at the Austrian Embassy in Washington, D.C., that Dr. Bergman was born in Austria and spent her childhood in Vienna before World War II. This program trains psychoanalysts to observe newborns in their natural setting, the home, and to be a presence for the new parents. Providing support and encouragement to new mothers and parents has long been a part of the health care system in European developed countries but is a recent development in this country. It is both preventive and a clinical service, if needed.

The Zero to Three Organization, located in Washington, D.C., is a multidisciplined organization that has influenced policy with regard to the welfare of children. The early intervention program is a national program that provides therapy for children between the ages of zero to three; this treatment is offered at no cost to the families. Occupational therapy, physical therapy, and language therapy are offered to repair developmental delays and to promote competent functioning as these children grow. Those of us who are psychoanalytically trained believe that, in addition to these therapies, it is within the context of the relationship between the child and parents that the grounding and soil is provided for these interventions to take hold. Returning to Little Hans, we might say that the help Freud gave Little Hans's father to parent his son was, therefore, the first parent-infant psychotherapy and was the seed from which so much has grown and flourished in our field.

Psychoanalytic theory and practice continues to be modified and expanded. I have focused on the research in the beginning of life, but this research has relevance for the individual throughout the life cycle. We can appreciate this in our current twenty-first-century world as we face disasters, terrorism, and the violence they bring. Psychoanalytic understanding, with its roots in the genius of Sigmund Freud, offers a beacon of light in dealing with these most difficult problems and their impact on children and families.

This day-long conference held in honor of Freud's 150th birthday at the Austrian Embassy offers a model for facing the challenge. The four national psychoanalytic organizations representing varying mental health disciplines have worked collaboratively and with mutual respect for the unique contributions each has made to psychoanalytic practice and thought. I would like to believe that this is what Freud had in mind when, in "The Question of Lay Analysis" he stated prophetically:

As a depth psychology, a theory of the mental unconscious, it can become indispensable to all the sciences which are concerned with the evolution of human civilization and its major institutions such as art, religion and the social order. It has already, in my opinion, afforded these sciences considerable help in solving their problems (p. 248).

NOTES

Ainsworth, M., M. Blehar, and E. Waters. (1978). *Patterns of Attachment: A Psychological Study of the Strange Situation.* Florence, KY: Lawrence Erlbaum Associates.

Fraiberg, S. H., E. Adelson, and V. Shapiro (1975). Ghosts in the nursery: A psychoanalytic approach to the problems of impaired infant-mother relationships. *Journal of the American Academy of Child Psychiatry* 14:3 (Summer 1975):387–421.

Freud, A., J. Goldstein, D. Burlingham, and A. Solnit. (1980) *Beyond the Best Interests of the Child.* New York: Free Press.

———. (1984) *Before the Best Interests of the Child.* New York: Free Press.

———. (1986). *In the Best Interests of the Child.* New York: Free Press.

Freud, S. (1909). Analysis of a Phobia in a Five Year Old Boy. *SE* 10:5–148.

———. (1925–1926). *The Question of Lay Analysis. SE* 20:248.

Mahler, M., F. Pine, and A. Bergman (1975). *Psychological Birth of the Human Infant: Symbiosis and Individuation.* London: Hutchinson.

Richmond, M. E. (1917). *Social Diagnosis.* Baltimore: The Russell Sage Foundation.

Silverman, M. (1980). A fresh look at the case of Little Hans. In M. Kanzer and J. Glenn (eds.), *Freud and His Patients* (pp. 95–120). Northvale, NJ: Jason Aronson.

"The Analytic Revelation Is a Revolutionary Force"*

Thomas Aichhorn

Let me start my comment with a quotation I found in the Anna Freud Collection in the archives of the Library of Congress here in Washington. In 1946 the Swiss psychoanalyst Philipp Sarasin—at this time member of the board of the International Psychoanalytical Association (IPA)—wrote to Anna Freud: "Concerning IPA and psycho-analysis the most important issue to me seems to be that Professor [Freud] is not among the living any more. His achievements in its totality lie in front of us. . . . The task of IPA is to pass on Freud's legacy to the next generation. It remains a fact that everybody interprets psycho-analysis in its own way. Those different interpretations represent the totality of Freud's work. But never the less we must not lose sight of his most fundamental idea which is the concept of *infantile sexuality*. This concept allows keeping the inner unity of IPA—notwithstanding splitting into various small fractions."[1]

In February 1920 Freud writes to Ernest Jones that a colleague had given him a book of Havelock Ellis as a present: "containing an essay on ψA or rather on my personality which is the most refined and amiable form of resistance and repudiation calling me a great artist in order to injure the validity of our scientific claims [which is all wrong, *I am sure in a few decades my name will be wiped away and our results will last*]."[2] [Italics added.] This prediction, the forgetting of Freud's name for the sake of psychoanalysis' scientific validity, has not yet been fulfilled. The fact that psychoanalysis has remained closely connected to Freud's name has different reasons. On the one hand because the reproduction of psychoanalysis, that is, psychoanalysts,

---

* Thomas Mann, 1936.

does not only occur through a theoretic-practical education, whose learning-processes take place within the medium of basic general knowledge, but also through training-analysis, which refers back to Freud's enigmatic messages.[3] On the other hand, Freud, whom Michel Foucault counts among the initiators of discursive practices, has radically shifted an entire mode of thinking. Between the initiation of psychoanalysis by Freud and its ulterior transformations there exists the fundamental heterogenity that overshadows the initiation of a discursive practice which is necessarily detached from its later developments and transformations and so the call for a "Return to the Source," namely to Freud, is going to be made loud with unavoidable necessity again and again. Foucault writes:

> If we return, it is not the result of accident or incomprehension. In effect, the act of initiation is such in its essence, that it is inevitably subjected to its own distortions; that which displays this act and derives from it is, at the same time, the root of its divergences and travesties. This nonaccidental omission must be regulated by precise operations that can be situated, analyzed and reduced in a return to the act of initiation. [. . .] In addition, it is always a return to a text in itself, specifically, to a primary and unadorned text with particular attention to those things registered in the interstices of the text, its gaps and absences. We return to those empty spaces that have been masked by omission or concealed in a false and misleading plenitude.[. . .] A last feature of these returns is that they tend to reinforce the enigmatic link between an author and his works. A text has an inaugurative value precisely because it is the work of a particular author and our returns are conditioned by this knowledge."[4]

What Foucault describes here complies well with the work Jean Laplanche is doing with his *New Foundations for Psychoanalysis*.[5]

In Freud's "Psychoanalysis and Libido Theory" from 1923 one finds the definition of psychoanalysis that has since been acknowledged as authoritative by the international psychoanalytical scientific community and has become a part of their common ground:

> Psycho-Analysis is the name (1) of a procedure for the investigation of mental processes [in German: *seelischer Vorgänge*, which means *psychic* processes!] which are almost inaccessible in any other way, (2) of a method (based upon that investigation) for the treatment of neurotic disorders and (3) of a collection of psychological information obtained along those lines, which is gradually being accumulated into a new scientific discipline."[6]

Freud initially saw himself as a researcher who studied phenomena that he had identified as psychic dysfunctions, later he claimed to have developed a general theory of the inner life—encompassing the "normal" psyche as well—and to be the founder of a new science. He did not consider the therapeutic application to be his most important contribution. Freud writes:

> I have told you that psycho-analysis began as a method of treatment; but I did not want to commend it to your interest as a method of treatment but on account of the truths it contains, on account of the information it gives us about what concerns human beings most of all—their own nature—and on account of the connections it discloses between the most different of their activities. As a method of treatment it is one among many, though, to be sure, primus *inter pares*."[7]

Freud was able to draw his conclusions because he questioned traditional values and suspended those seemingly normal dichotomies—powerful in both society and the subject—of good/evil, beautiful/ugly, sick/healthy, and normal/abnormal for his studies. He did not see these categories as self-evident but analyzed their genesis and opened areas for science that could be claimed from the realm of magic and religion. As Otto Fenichel writes, this was the main reason why psychoanalysis received other quantities and a different quality of resistance than other disciplines of science. For Freud studied the psychic reality without any reservation just as he did with physical occurrences: "he was able to witness circumstances that, although in plain sight had not been recognized before, infantile sexuality being an example," as Fenichel writes.[8] In that respect, Freud's psychoanalysis plays an important role in the formation of a liberal way of thinking as a general cultural attitude that confronts religious prejudice but also a certain materialism—that denies definitely existing psychic phenomena—with the ideals of pure reason and the unprejudiced examination of reality. Therefore all modern, pseudo-rational ideologies that promise bliss and happiness to their followers must face psychoanalysis—where any aspirations to omnipotence must undergo rational criticism—adversely by principle. Such ideologies draw their seductive powers from the fact that humans are born more helpless than other mammals and have learned that in a state of fear and helplessness a seemingly omnipotent force from the outside world comes to their aid. This force represents attempts at healing that seem to revoke the original, incurable trauma, the distress of helpless isolation, something that is bound to return later and even more forcefully on a collective scale. Indeed, any form of psychoanalytic work is characterized by its fundamental renouncement of power and it's acknowledgement of subjects as subjects.

Within the given limits of my comment here I'm unable to specify this any closer, but Freud suspected that his findings would be exposed to continuous threats. He distrusted both his followers—psychoanalysts—and the general culture in this regard. He foresaw a disfigurement, watering down and destruction of psychoanalysis caused by the society but also by his successors, who through an inherent human resistance could not bear the frightening truths that he had uncovered. With the establishment in 1910 of the IPA—as questionable as it is for a work in progress—he wanted to prevent misuse of psychoanalysis. He writes: "There should be some headquarters whose business it would be to declare: All this nonsense is nothing to do with analysis; this is not psycho-analysis."[9] In the following months and years many psychoanalytic societies were founded around the world. Freud's hope that these societies would follow the path he had led was disappointed however. While he had had to face adversity and slander from his opponents from the very beginning for his so-called overestimation of the importance of sexuality in psychic processes, he now had to experience similar rejection from many people—only beginning with Adler and Jung—who had been closely associated with him for some time. The issue always revolved and revolves around Freud's sexual theory, around his insight that sexuality plays the decisive role in the human unconscious, which is, as Laplanche writes "irrémédiablement sexuel."[10] Freud's sexual theory was and still is euphemized and ignored even by analysts, as though it were a foolish notion or a youthful misapprehension that can easily be neglected. And yet it is this very same result of Freud's sexual theory, which represents the source and foundation of psychoanalytical experience and treatment. Psychical symptoms—but also creativity—are attributable to sexuality. Blockages and fears can, if they are reactivated in transference, be solved, and using the example of dreams and parapraxes, Freud was able to prove the universality of the psychical mechanisms he had discovered. Freud's truly revolutionary insight was the discovery of infantile sexuality—determined by the drive and rooted in the It and therefore inaccessible to any direct observation—and another aspect of sexuality that is, similarly to animals, controlled by instinct. This instinct only emerges with puberty depending on the organism's process of maturation. While human sexuality expresses itself through the body, it is at the same time intimately connected with the individual's personal history, with the diversity of his desires.

I would like to close my comment on this discussion with a quote from the speech that Thomas Mann held in the Konzerthaus (concert hall) in Vienna on May 8, 1936, honoring Freud's eightieth birthday:

> Freud is of the opinion that the significance of psycho-analysis as a science of the unconscious will in the future far outrank its value as a therapeutic method. But even as a science of the unconscious it is a therapeutic method, in grand style, a method overarching the individual case. Call this, if you choose, a poet's utopia; but the thought is after all not unthinkable that the resolution of our great fear and our great hate, their conversion into a different relation to the unconscious which shall be more the artist's, more ironic and yet not necessarily ir-

reverent, may one day be due to the healing effect of this very science. The analytic revelation is a revolutionary force. With it a blithe scepticism has come into the world, a mistrust that unmasks all the schemes and subterfuges of our souls. Once roused and on alert, it cannot be put to sleep again. It infiltrates life, undermines its raw naiveté, takes from it the strain of its own ignorance, de-emotionalizes it, as it were, inculcates the taste for understatement, as the English call it—for the deflated rather than for the inflated word, for the cult which exerts its influence by moderation, by modesty. Modesty—what a beautiful word! [. . .] May we hope that this may be the fundamental temper of that more blithely objective and peaceful world which the science of the unconscious may be called to usher in?"[11]

As Freud's biographer Max Schur[12] reports, Thomas Mann's speech was not only understood as an homage to Freud but as an unmistakable challenge to the forces of a fundamental understanding and as a vehement plea for resistance against the national-socialist threat that Austria was then subjected to. It was understood as a praise of individual rights, a scientific view of the world and the power of the mind, the power of that intellect which by comparison to the power of religious and political ideologies may seem weak. And, as Freud wrote in *The Future of an Illusion*:

We may insist as often as we like that man's intellect is powerless in comparison with his instinctual life [kraftlos im Vergleich zum menschlichen Triebleben]. [. . .] Nevertheless, there is something peculiar about this weakness. The voice of the intellect is a soft one, but it does not rest till it has gained a hearing. Finally, after a countless succession of rebuffs, it succeeds. This one of the few points in which one may be optimistic about the future of mankind, but it is in itself a point of no small importance. [. . .] The primacy of the intellect lies, it is true, in a distant, distant future, but probably not in an infinitely distant one."[13]

Of course we now know that the influence Freud and his followers had has yet remained marginal in the course of history. There can be no knowledge that transcends into the future, we can only hope but never know absolutely whether people in the twenty-first century will respond to the message that Freudian psychoanalysis represents—namely to learn to bear the truths about ourselves without reservation—and finally to be ready to work on the fundamentals of a "more blithely objective and peaceful world".

NOTES

1. Ph. Sarasin to A. Freud, letter 11.2.1946. (Original: Anna-Freud Collection, Library of Congress, Washington, D.C.).

2. Freud, S. (1993e [1908–1939]). *Letters Sigmund Freud—Ernest Jones, 1908–1939*. Frankfurt am Main: S. Fischer Verlag, S. 370.

3. Gondek, H-D. (1998). "La séance continue" Jacques Derrida und die Psychoanalyse. In *Jacques Derrida Vergessen wir nicht—die Psychoanalyse!* Frankfurt am Main: edition suhrkamp, S. 182f.

4. Foucault, M. (1969). What is an author? In: *Language, Countermemory, Practice*. Ithaca, NY: Cornell University Press 1980: 113–38, p. 135f.

5. Laplanche, J. (1987). *New Foundations for Psychoanalysis*. Oxford: Blackwell, 1989.

6. Freud, S. (1923a). Two Encyclopaedia Articles; (A): Psycho-Analysis. *SE* 18: 235–59, p. 235.

7. Freud, S. (1933a). New Introductory Lectures on Psycho-Analysis. *SE* 22, p. 156.

8. Fenichel, O. *119 Rundbriefe*. Frankfurt am Main: Stroemfeld Verlag 1998; p. 922.

9. Freud, S. (1914d). On the History of the Psycho-Analytic Movement. *SE* 14: 7–66, p. 43.

10. Laplanche, J. (2006). *L'après-coup*. Problématique VI. Paris: PUF, p. 6.

11. Mann, Th. (1936). Freud and the Future. *International Journal of Psycho-Analysis* 37 (1956): 106-15, p. 114.

12. Schur, M. (1972). *Sigmund Freud Leben und Sterben*. Frankfurt am Main: Suhrkamp Verlag, 1973, p. 566.

13. Freud, S. (1927c). The Future of an Illusion. *SE* 21: 5-56, p. 53.

About the Editors

Joseph P. Merlino, MD, MPA, is immediate past president of the American Academy of Psychoanalysis and Dynamic Psychiatry, one of the nation's four major psychoanalytic organizations. He is director of psychiatry and behavioral health at Queens Hospital Center in New York City and clinical professor of psychiatry at the Mt. Sinai School of Medicine. Dr. Merlino is also adjunct professor of psychiatry and behavioral sciences at New York Medical College, where he is also supervising and training analyst. He is a distinguished fellow of the American Psychiatric Association, a fellow of The American Academy of Psychoanalysis and Dynamic Psychiatry, and a member of the prestigious Group for the Advancement of Psychiatry and the American College of Psychiatrists. He is chair of the board of directors of the Opportunity Charter School in Harlem, New York. Dr. Merlino is coeditor of *American Psychiatry & Homosexuality: An Oral History* (2007).

Marilyn S. Jacobs, PhD, ABPP, is a clinical psychologist and psychoanalyst in private practice in Los Angeles, California. In addition to providing psychoanalytic psychotherapy, Dr. Jacobs specializes in medical psychoanalysis, the treatment of patients with pain disorders, and consultations with physicians about medical care decision making. She is a training and supervising psychoanalyst and senior member at the Institute of Contemporary Psychoanalysis in Los Angeles. She holds the appointment of assistant clinical professor at the David Geffen School of Medicine at UCLA Medical Center. Dr. Jacobs is an active member of Division 39 (Psychoanalysis) of the American Psychological Association, where she has served as secretary to the board of directors. She has a longstanding interest in political psychoanalysis and is the author of *American Psychology in the Quest for Nuclear Peace* (1987).

Judy Ann Kaplan, MSW, BCD-P, is immediate past president and a former national study group member of the American Association for Psychoanalysis in Clinical Social Work (AAPCSW) and a distinguished practitioner in social work of the National Academy of Practice. She is a faculty member and supervisor at the Institute for Psychoanalytic Training and Research (IPTAR) and a faculty member, training and supervising analyst, and senior member at the National Psychological Association for Psychoanalysis (NPAP). She is a fellow of the International Psychoanalytic Association (IPA), a member of the Confederation of Independent Psychoanalytic Societies (CIPS), and past president of the Council of Psychoanalytic Psychotherapists (CPP). Ms. Kaplan is the author of numerous journal articles and a contributor to the *Psychodynamic Diagnostic Manual* (2006). She is in private practice in New York City.

K. Lynne Moritz, MD, is president of the American Psychoanalytic Association and a member of the board of representatives of the International Psychoanalytical Association. She is also clinical professor of psychiatry and human behavior at St. Louis University School of Medicine. Dr. Moritz is former director of the St. Louis Psychoanalytic Institute, where she is a training and supervising analyst. Dr. Moritz has been an activist in both state and federal legislative affairs, was president of the District Branch of the American Psychiatric Association, and was liaison from the American Psychiatric Association to the American Medical Association.

About the Contributors

Thomas Aichhorn is a social pedagogue and member of the Vienna Psychoanalytical Society. He has published about the theories of psychoanalysis, especially about the works of Jean Laplanche, and the history of psychoanalysis, in particular the history of the Psychoanalytical Society.

César Alfonso, MD, currently holds a teaching appointment at Columbia University College of Physicians and Surgeons. His clinical interests include the treatment of anxiety and depressive disorders in persons with concomitant medical illness; medical ethics; combining psychopharmacology with psychoanalytic and psychodynamic psychotherapy; and the psychoanalytic treatment of artists and creative individuals. Dr. Alfonso is a Fellow of the Academy of Psychosomatic Medicine, The New York Academy of Medicine, and of the American Academy of Psychoanalysis. He has been active in the American Academy of Psychoanalysis, serving as an officer for six years and as chair of various committees such as the Transcultural Psychiatry Study Group. Dr. Alfonso is an associate editor and book review editor of the *Journal of the American Academy of Psychoanalysis*.

Harold Blum, MD, is a clinical professor of psychiatry and training analyst at New York University School of Medicine, Department of Psychiatry. He also is executive director of the Sigmund Freud Archives at the Library of Congress and past editor-in-chief of the *Journal of the American Psychoanalytic Association*. Dr. Blum is past vice president of the International Psychoanalytical Association. He is the author of more than 140 psychoanalytic papers and several books; recipient of numerous awards and lectureships including the inaugural Sigourney Award, Mahler, Hartmann, and Lorand

Prizes; S. Freud lectures in New York, London, Vienna and Frankfurt; A. Freud, Hartmann, Brill, Friend and Sperling Lectures, two plenary addresses to the American Psychoanalytic Association. He has been chair of three symposia on psychoanalysis and art held in Florence, Italy.

Katherine Brunkow, MSW, is a clinical social worker and psychoanalyst. She earned her MSW at Catholic University and is a graduate of the Advanced Psychotherapy Program of the Washington School of Psychiatry. She completed analytic training at the Washington Psychoanalytic Institute, where she is now a supervising and training analyst. Her paper "Working with Dreams of Survivors of Violence," won the Gary O. Morris Research Prize and became a chapter in the book *Fostering Healing and Growth*. She serves on the clinical faculties of the Clinical Social Work Institute, the Modern Perspectives on Psychotherapy Program, and the George Washington University Psychiatry Residency. She has been a mental health consultant to the Peace Corps for twenty-five years, with overseas assignments in fifteen countries.

Jaine Darwin, PsyD, is past president of the Division of Psychoanalysis (39) of the American Psychological Association. She is faculty and supervising analyst at the Massachusetts Institute for Psychoanalysis as well as a member of their board of directors. She is a clinical instructor in psychology, Department of Psychiatry, Harvard Medical School, and a clinical supervisor at the Victims of Violence Program at the Cambridge Health Alliance. She is codirector of SOFAR: Strategic Outreach to Families of All Reservists, a pro bono program providing mental health services to families of U.S. soldiers in the Reserves and National Guard who are serving in Afghanistan, Iraq, and Kuwait. She is also a board member of the Psychoanalytic Couples and Family Institute of New England (PCFINE). She maintains a private practice in psychoanalysis and psychotherapy in Cambridge, Massachusetts.

William Granatir, MD, was a U.S. Army Air Corps Captain M.C. from August 1942 to January 1946, was two years in ETO, and awarded the soldier's medal in January 1945. From April 1946 to June 1948, he was resident in psychiatry at St. Elizabeth's Hospital. From June 1948 to June 1950, he was director of the Washington Institute of Mental Hygiene. He was training in psychoanalysis at Washington Psychoanalytic Institute, and training and supervising analyst in 1964. He is certified by the American Psychoanalytic Association. Dr. Granatir retired in June 1992. Since then, he has volunteered in Washington, D.C., public schools and established a consultation project. With Ms. Sheila Holt, a school counsellor, he established a pilot demonstration in a school with the assistance of graduate students in professional psychology and residents at St. Elizabeth's. He has worked successfully with

Mary Gardner Jones in a lobbying group to promote a school-based mental health program in D.C. schools. In 2001, a school-based program with mental health professionals was established in forty-six schools. He retired from this program in 2002.

Sheila Hafter Gray, MD, is a teaching analyst in the Baltimore-Washington Institute for Psychoanalysis and adjunct professor of psychiatry in the Uniformed Services University of the Health Sciences. She was formerly president of the American Academy of Psychoanalysis, and now serves as parliamentarian of the American Psychoanalytic Association and secretary of the Accreditation Council on Psychoanalytic Education, and on the Steering Committee on Practice Guidelines of the American Psychiatric Association.

John Kafka, MD, is a training and supervising analyst at the Washington Psychoanalytic Institute and a clinical professor of psychiatry and behavioural sciences at the George Washington University School of Medicine. He is the former president of the Washington Psychoanalytic Society and former chair of the education committee, Washington Psychoanalytic Institute. Other positions he has held include: vice president (2 terms) of the International Psychoanalytical Association; chair and cochair of the IPA Committee for Eastern Europe; member, IPA, East European Committee of the European Federation, and advisor of the Han Groen Prakken Eastern European Institute (PIEE). He is currently chair of the Moscow Sponsoring Committee for two Moscow psychoanalytic study groups. He has been active for over twenty years developing psychoanalysis in East Europe.

L. Gordon Kirschner, MD, is a physician, psychiatrist, and psychoanalyst, and maintains a private practice in Washington, D.C. He is a faculty member of the Washington School of Psychiatry and an assistant clinical professor at George Washington University Department of Psychiatry. Dr. Kirschner is a member of the Washington Psychoanalytic Society, the American Psychoanalytic Society, and the International Psychoanalytic Society, and of the Academy of Psychoanalysis and Dynamic Psychiatry. He has a special interest in treatment of psychic trauma that has led him deep in the study of affective neuroscience, that is, a focus on brain science with emphasis on emotional processes. He has taught both Freud's clinical technique and contemporary brain science. Additionally, he has an interest in art and aesthetics that informs his studies of all forms of human expressive processes.

James Kleiger, PsyD, ABPP, a diplomate in clinical psychology and practicing psychoanalyst, Dr. Kleiger is president-elect of the Baltimore-Washington Society for Psychoanalysis and a teaching analyst in the Baltimore-Washington Institute for Psychoanalysis. As coordinator of the Postgraduate

Psychoanalytic Seminar, Dr. Kleiger has attempted to gather internationally known analysts to present their work to members of our psychoanalytic community. Formerly the director of psychology training at the Menninger Clinic in Topeka, Kansas, Dr. Kleiger is the author of *Disordered Thinking and the Rorschach* (1999). He has written and presented extensively on psychoanalytic perspectives of psychological assessment.

Edith Kurzweil, PhD, a sociologist, is the former editor of *Partisan Review* and university professor emeritus of Adelphi University. Among her books are *The Age of Structuralism: Levi-Strauss to Foucault* (1980), *Italian Entrepreneurs: Success out of Chaos* (1983), *The Freudians: A Comparative Perspective* (1989), *Freudians and Feminists* (1995) and *Nazi Laws and Jewish Lives. Letters from Vienna* (1999, 2005). She received the National Endowment of Humanities medal in 2003.

Nancy McWilliams, PhD, teaches at the Graduate School of Applied and Professional Psychology at Rutgers, the State University of New Jersey. She is author of *Psychoanalytic Diagnosis: Understanding Personality Structure in the Clinical Process* (1994), *Psychoanalytic Case Formulation* (1999), and *Psychoanalytic Psychotherapy: A Practitioner's Guide* (2004), and is associate editor of the *Psychodynamic Diagnostic Manual* (2006). She is president-elect of the Division of Psychoanalysis (39) of the American Psychological Association, associate editor of the *Psychoanalytic Review*, and on the editorial board of *Psychoanalytic Psychology*.

Michael Meagher, MD, is adult, child, and adolescent psychoanalyst and teaching analyst at the Baltimore/Washington Psychoanalytic Institute and Society. He is psychiatric consultant to the Foundation School, a special education school for severely emotionally disturbed children and adolescents.

J. David Miller, MD, is a psychiatrist and psychoanalyst in private practice in Washington, D.C. He is currently the director of the Washington Psychoanalytic Institute, where he is a supervising and training analyst. He is also clinical professor of psychiatry at the George Washington University, having taught psychiatry residents there for many years. His prior educational background includes a B.A. from Harvard College, magna cum laude in history and literature, and medical school and psychiatry residency at Columbia University. He also has a master's degree in public health/community psychiatry from Columbia University. Dr. Miller has long been interested in the application of psychoanalysis to other domains, first to the area of consultation in the community, where he has worked with emergency room staff, police, and school counsellors. In more recent years he has integrated his love of the arts with his psychoanalytic studies. He has thought not only about applications of psychoanalysis to the arts, but about how we may study psychoanalysis and the arts together, in an interdisciplinary approach that enlarges our understanding of both fields.

Stanley Palombo, MD, practices psychoanalysis in Washington, D.C. He is the author of *Dreaming and Memory: A New information-Processing Model* and *The Emergent Ego: Complexity and Coevolution in the Psychoanalytic Process*. He has served on the governing boards of the American Academy of Psychoanalysis and the American College of Psychoanalyst.

Miriam Pierce, CSW, BCD, was program chair for the NMCOP 2004 Conference. Currently, she is vice president of the New York School for Psychoanalytic Psychotherapy and Psychoanalysis and chair of its child and adolescent program. She is also a member of the New York Freudian Society, where she graduated from its infant toddler program and currently is a supervisor. Ms. Pierce is also a member of the Institute for Psychoanalytic Training and Research, the International Psychoanalytical Association, and the American Psychoanalytic Association. She is in the private practice of psychoanalysis with adults and psychotherapy with infants, toddlers, and their parents in New York City.

David Ramirez, PhD, ABPP, earned his doctorate from the University of Texas, Austin. He did his psychoanalytic training at the Philadelphia School of Psychoanalysis. He is the director of Psychological Services, Swarthmore College, Swarthmore, Pennsylvania. He is past president of Division of Psychoanalysis (39) and president of the American Psychological Association.

Richard Ruth, PhD, is associate professor of clinical psychology at the Center for Professional Psychology, George Washington University, and on the faculty and steering committee of the child and adolescent psychotherapy program at the Washington School of Psychiatry, both in Washington, D.C. He is also in the private practice of psychoanalysis and clinical psychology. He has published in the areas of cross-cultural clinical psychology, disability, and trauma.

Ann-Louise Silver, MD, is a past president of the American Academy of Psychoanalysis and Dynamic Psychiatry and chaired its scientific programs committee for six years. She is the president of the U.S. chapter of the International Society for the Psychological Treatments of the Schizophrenias and Other Psychoses (www.isps-us.org). She is on the faculties of the Uniformed Services University of the Health Sciences, the University of Maryland

School of Medicine, the Washington Psychoanalytic Institute, the Washington School of Psychiatry, and is a civilian consultant at the Walter Reed Army Medical Center. She edited the book *Psychoanalysis and Psychosis*, and edited with Harvey Schwartz *Illness in the Analyst: Implications for the Therapeutic Relationship*. She founded the Columbia (Maryland) Academy of Psychodynamics. She chaired the Clinical Sándor Ferenczi Conference, held August 2–6, 2006 in Baden-Baden, celebrating Ferenczi's and Groddeck's friendship and collaboration. For twenty-five years, she was on the medical staff of Chestnut Lodge in Rockville, Maryland. She is in the private practice of psychiatry and psychoanalysis in Columbia, Maryland.

Golnar Simpson, PhD, is dean and founding dean of the Clinical Social Work Institute in Washington, D.C., and practices clinical social work in McLean, Virginia. She received her MSW from Virginia Commonwealth University and her Ph.D. from Catholic University of America. Dr. Simpson is a distinguished practitioner of the National Academies of Practice and has served as the chair of Social Work Academy of Practice. She has also served as the president of the National Clinical Social Work Association. Dr. Simpson's teaching and writing include various aspects of clinical social work theory, practice, and education. She has a particular interest in the integration of neuroscience research into social work theory and practice and lectures widely on this and other clinical social work topics at the local and national levels.

Helmut Strutzmann, PhD, has owned the public relations agency, Multiart, since 1983. After earning his doctorate in drama, semiotics and fine arts, Helmut Strutzmann worked as a journalist for the ORF (Austrian Broadcasting Corporation), *Salzburger Nachrichten, Kronen Zeitung*, as well as a correspondent for Italian newspapers. The main focus of Multiart is on issues concerning public institutions and institutional public relations, public relations and the media, media consulting, public relations and the mobility and energy industry, online content management, culture and public relations and cultural projects, also in terms of conceptual design and implementation. Helmut Strutzmann is an instructor at the Technical College for Communications and Marketing in Vienna and author of numerous books on literature and literary criticism, art history, and sociology.

Audrey Thayer Walker, MSS, is a distinguished practitioner at the National Academy of Practice (Social Work). She is an adjunct associate professor at George Washington University Medical School, Department of Psychiatry and Behavioural Sciences. In 2005, she received the Day Garrett Award for significant contributions to the field of social work. Between 1993 and 2005, she had a part-time faculty at Georgetown University Counselling and Psychiatric Services. She is also a part-time faculty consultant/educational policy advisory committee at the Clinical Social Work Institute, Inc., in Washington, D.C. She was the area chair of the national membership committee on psychoanalysis in clinical social work for the Washington, D.C./Baltimore area from 1996 to 2006. She has a full-time clinical social work practice in Washington, D.C., and is a clinician, educator, consultant, and supervisor.

Pratyusha Tummala-Narra, PhD, is a clinical psychologist and chair of the multicultural concerns committee of Division of Psychoanalysis of the American Psychological Association. Dr. Tummala-Narra is the founder and former director of the Asian Mental Health Clinic at the Cambridge Hospital, and the former director of the trauma and loss program at the Georgetown University Hospital. After relocating to Michigan in 2005, she has been a clinical supervisor at the University of Michigan Psychological Clinic, and is currently adjunct professor at the Michigan School for Professional Psychology. She also has a private practice in Farmington Hills, Michigan. Dr. Tummala-Narra's primary scholarly interests include psychological trauma, multicultural psychology, and psychoanalytic psychotherapy.

Eli Zaretsky, PhD, is professor of history at the New School for Social Research in New York City. He is the author of *Secrets of the Soul. A Social and Cultural History of Psychoanalysis*, translated into six languages, including German, where it appeared as *Freuds Jahrhundert*. He is also the author of *Capitalism, the Family and Personal Life* and the editor of *The Polish Peasant in Europe and America*.